Ethnicity, Class and the Struggle for State Power in Liberia

I0110169

Eghosa E Osaghae
University of Ibadan
Nigeria

Monograph Series 1/96

The CODESRIA Monograph Series is published to stimulate debate, comments, and further research on the subjects covered. The Series will serve as a forum for works based on the findings of original research, which however are too long for academic journals but not long enough to be published as books, and which deserve to be accessible to the research community in Africa and elsewhere. Such works may be case studies, theoretical debates or both, but they incorporate significant findings, analyses, and critical evaluations of the current literature on the subjects in question.

Ethnicity, Class and the Struggle for State Power in Liberia

Typeset and printed by CODESRIA

CODESRIA Monograph Series is distributed free of charge to African research institutes and to other institutes within our exchange programme. Single copies can be obtained at US$8. For information, please contact:

CODESRIA
P.O. Box 3304
Dakar/Senegal

CODESRIA Monograph Series

ISBN 1-904855-16-4

CODESRIA gratefully acknowledges the support of the Swedish Agency for Research Cooperation (SAREC), the International Development Research Centre (IDRC), the Ford Foundation, the Rockefeller Foundation, the Danish International Development Agency (DANIDA) and the Norwegian Ministry of Foreign Affairs.

Contents

The Author

Eghosa E Osaghae has been teaching political science in the University of Ibadan since 1982. A scholar with a wide range of academic interests, he has published widely on ethnicity, federations, political theory and agriculture. His publications include *Federal Character and Federalism in Nigeria* (Ibadan:Heinemann) which he coedited with Peter Ekeh, *The Federal Solution in Nigeria* (Lagos:Malthouse), he edited *Between State and Civil Society in Africa* (Dakar:CODESRIA).

Preface

In spite of the popularity of ethnic explanations in Africa, ethnicity remains heavily under-studied in several countries. The case of Liberia is particularly lamentable because the country possesses features which ought to make it attractive to scholars of ethnicity. Liberia is Africa's oldest Republic, having been declared a sovereign Republic in 1847; her circumstances present an ethnic scenario which is unique in Africa — it began as a settler colony in which a small group of Americo-Liberians, who are today known as 'Congoes', constituting less than 3 per cent of the country's population established ethclass hegemonic rule which survived for over a century; most of Liberia's ethnic groups are cross-border groups whose kith an kin are in neighbouring countries. Liberia has been battlefield of fierce struggles for power which culminated into a civil war in 1989; and Liberia has one of the weakest and most foreign-controlled national economies in Africa. These features make a study of ethnicity in the country something which can potentially supply answers to the age-long questions about the relationship between the age of a country and the capability to manage ethnic conflicts, the implications for ethnicity of foreign control of the economy, the consequences of prolonged hegemonic rule on inter-ethnic relations and the implications of cross-border ethnicity.

Yet, the study of ethnicity in Liberia, like the study of most other subjects in the country, is in an appalling state. This is especially true of the situation of indigenous Liberian groups (hereafter referred to as African-Liberians). The reason for this lies in the misconception that analysing the Americo-Liberians was the relevant key to understanding the country's political reality, which is something the literature on Liberia up until the late 1970s is most guilty of. Analysis of African-Liberians was often tucked in somewhere as an appendage. It was left entirely to the anthropologists and linguists to continue in their preservationist scholarship of analysing African-Liberians in terms of their responses to the modernisation stimuli elicited by Americo-Liberian elites. Consequently, once the Africans responded well and became incorporated into the country established by settlers for themselves, many reached the misleading conclusion that Liberia, like the United States of America, was on its way to becoming another melting pot. The coup of 1980 and the subsequent events that led to the civil war in 1989 jolted those Liberianists who were fixed to this view out of this fantasy. These events brought to clear focus, the fact that, in spite of its familiarity, so little is known about the ethnic situation in Liberia.

Now is the time to set about this knowledge, to re-examine conventional wisdom about Liberian politics. The present work is intended as a contribution to this endeavour.

I must admit that the ambition in writing on ethnic politics in Liberia cannot but be constrained. There is a dearth of materials on the country and it has not been possible for me to return to the country for fieldwork because of the prevailing atmosphere of tension and anxiety. Still, it is easy to see that the study of the ethnic situation needs urgent attention. I cannot lay claim to having exhausted all that the Liberian ethnic situation calls for, but my hope is that I have been able to generate relevant frameworks that will enable the proper questions to be asked. What I have tried to do, 'in specific terms, is to see how much of the cleavages which are supposed to have melted can be found in the current crisis of the country has gone through. For such a study, I found no more appropriate approach to the historical approach which reveals a great deal of the hidden continuities about the character of the Liberian state and society that culminated into the civil war.

In another sense, this little piece is the fulfilment of a desire which my academic instincts aroused the first time I arrived in Liberia but which was nearly aborted when I had to flee with my family from the civil war. I must thank CODESRIA for the opportunity it has offered for this fulfilment and Professor O. Nnoli, Coordinator of the Ethnic Conflict Network for assigning the Liberian task to me. I also must thank the Institut fur Africa-Kunde (Hamburg, Germany) which responded very positively to my enquiries on literature and Benson Osadolor of the Department of History at Ibadan and Don Williams of Political Science, Western New England College, Massachusetts who were of immense assistance in making relevant literature available to me at personal expense. Thanks are also due to Rev. William Kollie, former Chaplain of the Liberian Senate and other students of mine at the Babangida Graduate School of International Relations who helped to sharpen some of my thoughts on the Liberian situation. In this regard, also, I am grateful to Professor Bayo Adekanye of Department of Political Science at Ibadan and to all the participants at the Nairobi final Workshop for the Ethnic Conflicts in Africa network in November 1992. I am particularly grateful to Professor P. Anyang' Nyong'o, Professor G. K. Agyeman, Jacob Jaygbay and Professor Edward Oyuji for their very useful criticisms and comments which have emboldened the study. I express my gratitude to Victor Isumonah who read the manuscripts and offered useful advice and encouragement and Mrs. F. M. Awolaja, who was most diligent in typing the work.

Finally, it is to my wife, Amen, our darling Osahon and Noyosayi (who knew Liberia was not safe to arrive) who kept up with my long stays away from home and to Osarhieme, Osamudiamen and O. J. Offiong whom we were all in Liberia together, that I dedicate this work in testimony of our surviving the agonising days when the war came.

Ibadan, August 1993
Eghosa E. Osaghae

1 - Conceptualising the Ethnic Situation in Liberia

The ethnic situation, involving the character of ethnic groups and the conflicts among them, as well as their class, regional, racial, religious and other correlates and finally, the factors which make them politically salient, differs from one society to another. For this reason, I have argued elsewhere, attempts to universalise the concept of ethnicity, for all their scientific merits, must be treated with great caution because they tend to gloss over the peculiarities which make ethnicity in the United States of America, for example, different from ethnicity in Africa (Osaghae 1992). At the African level also, it is equally dangerous to universalise because of the contextual peculiarities which attend ethnicity in different countries. Variables such as the level of economic development and economic relations, the number and sizes of ethnic groups, the nature and linkages of cleavages, historical experiences, especially under colonial rule and the uses of ethnicity, are quite useful in explaining these differences. The great importance of contextual peculiarities makes it necessary for us to begin this study with a conceptualisation of the ethnic situation in Liberia which presents a rather unique case in Africa.

Ethnic Groups in Liberia

Unlike most countries in Africa, the ethnic situation in Liberia has historically involved not only primordially rooted ethnic groups, but also, the relationship between these groups which constitute the majority (98 per cent) and the minority (2 per cent) group which came as settlers, founded the country and, through self-perpetuating strategies, virtually monopolised power and privileges from 1847 when the country became independent until 1980. For a long time and, in several ways until today Americo-Liberian/African-Liberian relations constituted the hub of the ethnic situation in the country. This made the Liberian situation quite similar to other settler colonies in Africa but especially to South Africa where, like the Americo-Liberians, the whites have monopolised power and, through apartheid policies, denied the majority blacks of citizenship rights (Obatala 1973, for a comparison of South Africa and Liberia and Shick (1973) for a critique of this comparison). But unlike South Africa and other settler colonies, the Americo-Liberian settlers in Liberia were black, not white. In fact, both the 1847 and Second Republican constitutions forbade granting of citizenship to persons other than those belonging to the negro race. Moreover, unlike other settler colonies where membership of the privileged ranks is closed to blacks, the Americo-Liberian ranks were open to African-Liberians who, upon acquiring prescribed qualifications, were incorporated or assimilated. Although this process of assimilation was very slow, there was a significant number of non-settler 'Americo-Liberians' by the time the 1980 coup took place. Also, several years of inter-marriages have helped to blur part of the boundary lines.

How then should the ethnic situation in Liberia be analysed? Can we regard the Americo-Liberians as constituting an ethnic group? Extant analyses, in general, do not treat Americo-Liberian/African-Liberian relations in ethnic terms. The reason is partly historical and partly conceptual. Historically, just as in the rest of Africa, 'tribes' (which African-Liberian groups are called by Americo-Liberians) were defined, in a pejorative manner, as groups of 'uncivilised' people, different from 'civilised' Americo-Liberians. For example, Anderson (1952:2) asserts that the two distinct groups in Liberia are the aboriginal tribes, natives emerging from savagery and the highly cultured Americo-Liberians, the ruling class.[1]
North Americans and Western Scholars, used to such perjorativeness, have carried on in this manner, and the tendency has been to treat only conflicts among the African-Liberian groups, which dominated the post-1980 period as ethnic. At the conceptual level, because the Americo-Liberian group is not primordially rooted in terms of culture and language as the indigenous groups are; most analysts prefer to treat it as a class rather than an ethnic group or, worse still, a 'tribe'. This raises a major conceptual problem. If we are to treat the Americo-Liberians as a class and the African-Liberians as ethnic groups we would have to deal with two sets of analytical variables. On the other hand, if we take the easy way out and treat both in class terms, it would be difficult for us to properly analyse relations among African-Liberian groups (and even among Americo-Liberians).

To resolve this conceptual difficulty, Gordon's (1964) ethclass approach which was formulated to analyse situations in which there is an intersection of class and ethnic categories, immediately suggests itself. We can also borrow a leaf from analyses of the South-African situation which treat the white as an ethnic category as well as a class and race in relation both to

---

1   In fact, Anderson regarded only Americo-Liberians as Liberians.

themselves and the blacks (Van den Berghe 1967; Slabbert and Welsh 1979; Adam 1983). To be able to do this well, Slabbert and Welsh (1979:10) recommend that the ethnic group should be defined in the broadest terms:

> as a group that is bounded off from other comparable groups or population categories in the society by a sense of its difference which may consist in some combination of a real or mythical ancestry and a common culture and experience.

They then make the relevant point which suits our purpose quite well: 'Employed in a context of intergroup relations, this definition would cover groups that are physically or racially (or classly) different as well as those that are culturally different'.

Along these lines, we can regard the Americo-Liberian group as an ethnic category in addition to it being a class. The class dimension relates to the fact that Americo-Liberian/African-Liberian division also defines the stratification lines between the privileged group and the non-privileged groups. It is in this sense that Enloe (1973) has, for example, described the ethnic situation in Liberia as an instance of vertical ethnic differentiation in which social identification is synonymous with ethnicity and in which, for a long time, upward mobility required a change in ethnic identity through assimilation.[2] In addition to this, Americo-Liberians have always been major ethnic actors, even in cases where the conflicts appear to involve only African-Liberians. The so-called 'tribal wars' of the 19th century and the civil war which erupted in 1989 are two good examples. What the Americo-Liberians have done usually, is to manipulate ethnic differences in manners that are best described in divide and rule terms. Americo-Liberians are ethnic actors in another major, but more contemporary way. Over the years, through closer association and intermarriages with African-Liberians many American-Liberians have not only had part-indigenous parents, they have also affiliated themselves with ethnic groups and culture. Finally, in terms of core-territoriality which is one of the objective bases of ethnic groups in Africa (Otite 1990), the Americo-Liberians being concentrated mainly in the coastal counties — Montserrado, Maryland, Sinoe, Grand Bassa and Grand Cape Mount — constitute a distinct group apart from the other groups. This distinctiveness is reinforced and perpetuated in several ways as we shall discuss below. It is this conscious group perpetuation that has made class analysis attractive to many authors.

---

2   This was usually done through the adoption of an Americo-Liberian name.

The relationship between Americo-Liberians and African-Liberians has been characterised in other ways. One of these which was popular until the unification era of Tubman, was that it was racial, to emphasise the fact that Americo-Liberians, even though black, came from the 'new world' and also the fact, at the initial stage of settlement, that the dominant Americo-Liberians were really the mulattos not black settlers. Even if the latter point was valid at a point in the 19th century, the fact that the constitution granted citizenship only to 'negroes' meant that racial differentiation was never a serious point. In debunking the racial argument, a Liberian author has further written:

> Both historical experience and common sense seem to suggest that racial antagonisms are irreducible ... [because] the groups involved are so conspicuously different by virtue of their colour or physical features as to preclude any possibility of absorption or infiltration (Simpson 1961:85-86).

In other words, there is no racial differentiation amongst Liberians because, apart from being racially the same, the Americo-Liberian group was never a closed group.[3] Indeed, according to Buell (1965:749), no clear-cut physical distinction existed between the Americo-Liberians and African-Liberians, and this was continually made possible by an 'amazing process of amalgamation'. The same points have been advanced to debunk the characterisation of relations between Americo-Liberians and African-Liberians in caste terms (Lowenkopf 1976:15).

This leaves us then with the ethclass framework within which, we have said, the ethnic situation in the country will be analysed. We shall now proceed to examine the ethnic groups — their composition and character. But before doing so, two important points need to be emphasised. The first is that although the American/African Liberian division is a useful summary of the ethnic situation, the complexities of intra-group relations makes it a simplistic description. Indeed, there are as many conflicts within each category as there are between them, a fact we shall elaborate on below. Secondly, it is important to stress that in treating the Americo-Liberian group as an ethnic group like the others, we are not obliterating the objective differences between them. For instance, the monopoly of power and privileges which the Americo-Liberians had until 1980 cannot be explained simply in ethnic terms. Similarly, the quality of Americo-Liberian

---

3   The so-called openness of the group underplays the fact that African-Liberians were only admitted on terms prescribed by the Americo-Liberians. This made them a compradox segment of the ruling class, as I argue in Chapter 3.

ethnicity and that of African-Liberian ethnicity are not the same: the former was historically 'Western' and the latter 'primordial'. Hopefully, these differences would be made clearer as we examine the two ethnic categories.

The Americo-Liberians

As indicated earlier on, the most popular description of the Americo-Liberians is in terms of class. The reason is that, until 1980, they constituted the privileged or ruling class which pursued a deliberate policy of perpetuating itself through the instrument of the state. The origins of this 'class consciousness' which preserved their solidarity are an integral part of the country's history which we shall consider in chapter two. For our immediate purpose, what is important to know is that the Americo-Liberians established the Republic for themselves exclusively, in part to realise the promise of privileges which lured most of them from the United States of America to Liberia. Thus, for a long time, African-Liberians were not regarded as Liberians. Even when the time came for them to be integrated into the country, the Americo-Liberians were unwilling to relinquish their hold on power, preferring to admit African-Liberians into their ranks in trickles and on their own terms, as an internal comprador class. The Americo-Liberians were a small group which Liebenow (1969, 1987) describes as an interlocking family and (coastal) regional network that constituted a mere 1 per cent of the total population.[4] It was precisely because of this small size that they were neither willing to admit too many African-Liberians into their ranks nor to allow for an expansion of the political participation arena.[5]

The class treatment of the Americo-Liberians has tended to gloss over the fact that, historically, the Americo-Liberians were not a homogeneous group. Although the differences that existed amongst them have melted away rapidly over the years, their historical significance lies in the fact that they help to explain the character of Americo-Liberian domination and the fact that part of the seeds for the eventual overthrow of hegemonic rule lay within the Americo-Liberians themselves. In terms of how they came to

---

4   Hayman and Preece (1943) further describe them as 'a self-perpetuating cabal' or 'oligarchy'.

5   This is similar to the South African case. As we shall find out in Chapter 5, the major disadvantage the Americo-Liberians had after they lost control of power was their numerical inferiority.

5

settle in Liberia, the initial access they had to power and the inequalities amongst them, there were three distinct sub-groups in the hierarchically structured Americo-Liberian group. At the apex were the mulattos who were products of illicit sexual relationships between female black slaves and their owners in the United States of America. The mulattos were free-born American citizens who occupied the lowest rungs of the social ladder in the early 19th Century United States of America south and who were lured to Liberia by the promise that 'the virtuous and industrious were nearly sure to obtain... in a few years, to a style of comfortable living, which they might in vain hope for in the United States of America' (Gurley 1839:368). Akpan (1978:98) has also pointed to freedom from white oppression, intellectual, material and spiritual development, investment in African trade and spreading the gospel to the heathen as some of the other allurements. These points are important in explaining why the mulattos felt superior to the other settlers who were freed slaves and sought to dominate power at the early stages. Indeed, the Republican Party principally of mulattos, controlled the country from 1847 until 1870 when the first black President Edward James Roye was elected. The mulattos were quite a small group and settled mainly in Monrovia whose commercial, political and educational life they dominated using the Republican Party and the Masonic fraternity. They discriminated so much against other settlers that Edward Blyden was forced to resign from the Republican Party. The mulatto dynasty did not last for a long time because by the 1860s, they had been numerically eaten up by the black settlers whose True Whig Party (TWP) then took over the reins of power.[6] Subsequently, generations of intermarriages completely wiped out the mulatto distinction.

The next Americo-Liberian group was made up of the black freed slaves whose continued stay in the United States of America, the colonisation societies feared, was a threat to the white society; in fact, some of them were freed on the condition that they would return to Africa. However, not all the freed slaves came from the United States of America; a good number came from Barbados in the West Indies and Sierra-Leone. This group was numerically preponderant, an advantage which its members strengthened by joining forces with the other black freed slaves in the TWP to dominate power in the country continuously from 1884 till 1980. One distinct feature of the returnee freed slaves and freeborn mulattos was the importance

---

6   The TWP then ruled for an unbroken period of 102 years.

attached to familial ties which Liebenow (1969:16) attributes to their 'reaction against the cruel and recurrent disruption of the slave family and the status of illegitimacy for the products of mixed unions'. A similar explanation has been advanced by Ekeh (1990) for strong kinship ties amongst groups which were victims of slave trade.

At the lowest rung of the hierarchy were the recaptured slaves who were rescued from slave ships seized by the United States of America navy on the West African Coast and resettled in Liberia. These recaptured slaves who were called 'Congoes'[7] had not gone to the 'new world', but were treated by the Americo-Liberians as superior to the 'natives' because they settled around them and were quite receptive to 'civilised' apprenticeship. Lowenkopf (1976:13) has described them thus:

> Although a number of them mixed and inter-married with indigenous tribal people, the Congoes tended to attach themselves to American settlements often as agricultural employees. Through emulation of, and intermarriage with the Americans, the Congoes came to share the prerogatives — if not the status of the ruling group. One thing the Congoes had in their advantage was industry in farming, a vocation which the 'new world' settlers resented as part of the slave deal from which they had been freed. The wealth thus brought to them, their quick response to civilised ways, and the partnership they forged with the others in the TWP, all quickly made them acceptable to the Americo-Liberians.

In their relationship with African-Liberians who threatened their settlements for a long time, it was not difficult for the Americo-Liberians to paper over their differences. Furthermore, they felt superior to the African-Liberians and clung to their distinct marks of 'civilisation' which differentiated them: luxurious cars and houses, Western dress, literacy and fluency in English language, christianity, freemasonry, anglo-saxon names, etc. Where possible, they segregated themselves from the 'uncivilised' natives — in churches, in urban neighbourhoods at political meetings, and other gatherings (Jones 1962).[8] Finally, they held on to power and sought to perpetuate their domination. All these elements of 'class consciousness' are called forth to establish that they are a class, but as we have said, these

---

7   This was probably because many of these freed slaves were from the Congo. Today, the term has become a generalised reference to all Americo-Liberians by the indigenous people.

8   One major instrument of Americo-Liberian distinctiveness was the mason fraternities to which only they belonged.

elements also make them an ethnic category in relation to the African Liberians.

The question may now be asked, if the Americo-Liberian group which was overthrown from power in 1980 still exists. The popular view is that by the mid-1970s, the idea of the group was more a matter of historical significance than anything else due to what Buell (1965:749) calls an 'amazing process of amalgamation'. However, the events of the post 1980 period which eventually led to the civil war, and the patterns of involvement in that war, do not support the implied melting pot theory. On the contrary, the events indicated that the Americo-Liberian remains a critical self-serving group. What can be said, therefore, is that although the number of pure Americo-Liberians (i.e. without African-Liberian pedigree) faces possible extinction, there continues to be an Americo-Liberian ethnocentricity and conscious struggle for state power.

The final point to be made about the Americo-Liberians is that it was an open group which admitted few African-Liberians who possessed the requisite qualifications for assimilation. But this assimilation became significant only in the period beginning from the 1950s and, even so, it remained entirely on terms set by the Americo-Liberians. As Lowenkopf (1976:172) elaborates, up until 1980 when they were overthrown 'eminent tribesmen who held positions in the legislature, the government or TWP usually did so as a result of sponsorship (or at least acceptance) by older members of the elite. They (did not) hold independent political power, nor did they enjoy social partly with the older members of the elite'. It is for this reason that I have described the African-Liberian elite of the pre-1980 era as comprador.

The African-Liberians

When we turn to African-Liberians, we come to deal with ethnic groups such as are found in other parts of Africa whose relationships with one another, including the statuses that they have, have been transformed in the colonial process which, in this case, involved rule by the Americo-Liberians. However, the Americo-Liberian/African-Liberian framework of analysis prevented analysts from studying the relations among African-Liberian groups for a long time. This explains the very poor state of scholarship in this area, as the few anthropologists who have dominated it have yet to purge themselves of romanticist-preservationist biases which have everywhere made orthodox anthropological studies inadequate in

8

explaining present realities. The situation is so bad that even when the conflicts among African-Liberians in the post-1980 period practically replaced the ones between them and the Americo-Liberians, the building blocks of analysis — including especially, a knowledge of the ethnic groups themselves — remained rudimentary. For example, very little is known of the historical relationships between the Gio/Mano and the Krahn, the groups which were major actors in the civil war. There was so much concentration on ethnographical study and on treating African-Liberians as one group in relation to the Americo-Liberians, that relations amongst the former tended to be undermined. Surely, a lot more research is required in this area.

Like those elsewhere in Africa, indigenous ethnic groups in Liberia are defined in terms of objective criteria mainly, language, territory, culture and myth of common descent, as well as subjective criteria which involve in-group and out-group members relating on the basis of identity based on the objective criteria. Of these criteria, most authors agree that language has clearly been the most important for identifying ethnic groups in Africa (Nnoli 1978, 1989). The situation in Liberia is not different. On the basis of language mainly, the number of African-Liberian ethnic groups has been put variously at 16 (Shulze 1973; Clifford 1971; Schwab and Harley 1947; Marinelli 1964); 28 (Lowenkopf 1976); and 30 (Anderson 1952). The official and most widely used figure is 16, according to the 1962 Census figures (see Table 1). What accounts for the wide variations in the number is the famous problem faced by all students of ethnicity in Africa: whether or not to take a dialect or sub-group of a language group as an ethnic group on its own. This problem is made worse in the Liberian situation by the fact that in the absence of centralised state-societies, the basic unit of political organisation is the clan or chiefdom. This is indeed, the official position as a 'tribe' is defined by government as 'a body or number of clans having a name, a dialect, a government and a territory of its own'. Because these tribes are the units of local government, some of them are 'tribes' created by government (Anderson 1952; Roberts et al. 1972).[9] If we are to think of ethnic groups as political units, then of course, we would have over one hundred groups. For purposes of analysing intra-group relations, it is necessary to include such ethnic subdivisions in to the ethnic action-set

---

9   This is similar to the point made by Apthorpe (1965) about how colonial authorities in East
     Africa administratively created ethnic groups. It is rare however to find any such group
     which does not have a non-primordial basis. In the Liberian case, these so-called
     administratively 'created' tribes are actually the sub-units of larger ethnic groups.

(McEvoy 1977) but for our immediate purpose, ethnic groups are taken to be major language groups which, along with other objective criteria, provide the basis for political differentiation and behaviour. As we have said, there are officially 16 major groups and the remarkable thing about them is that although the Bassa and Kpelle are a little preponderant, the groups are small-sized and relatively balanced.

Table 1: Major Ethnic Groups in Liberia

Ethnic Group	Population (1974)	Percent
Kpelle	298,532	20.0
Bassa	214,143	14.0
Gio	130,360	9.0
Kru	121,414	8.0
Grebo	119,985	8.0
Mano	110,770	7.0
Loma	88,351	6.0
Krahn	71,177	5.0
Gola	67,819	4.0
Kissi	51,318	3.0
Mandingo	58,414	4.0
Vai	49,504	3.0
Gbandi	38,548	3.0
Belle	7,309	0.5
Dei	6,365	0.5
Mende	8,678	0.5
Americo-Liberian*	42,834	2.9
Others	2,299	0.2
Total	1,488,662	98.6

Source: Compiled by author.

* This is regarded as the segment of the population which has no ethnic affiliation.

The neat identification of the major ethnic groups belies the poor state of ethnographical research on Liberian groups. This is partly due to the fact that the Americo-Liberian colonialists or, before them, the American Colonisation Society (ACS) which founded the country had neither the means nor sufficient scholarly motivation, even if for the purpose of facilitating colonial rule, to undertake ethnographical studies as colonisers did in other parts of Africa. Subsequently, most of those who studied

Liberia were too pre-occupied with politics in a dual society to have time to study 'native' groups which, for the purposes of modernisation, were best left to antiquity. The few anthropological researches that have been undertaken have concentrated, in the framework of the social change for which neoclassical anthropology is famous, on those groups which have had the greatest contacts with the Americo-Liberians and/or which played prominent roles in Liberian history, like the Kru, Vai, Kpelle, Loma and Gbandi and other coastal groups. The under-study situation of the hinterland groups explains the confusions which still attend how to spell group names and define them. For example, there is a great deal of confusion over the identification of eastern Liberian ethnic groups which are variously called Dan, Ngere, Dan N'gere, Gio, Yacouba, Tien and so on (Holsoe 1976; Holsoe et. al. 1969; Murdock 1959). Similar confusions exist in the chiefdoms of Bopolu (Gola-Mandingo-Kpelle), Gibi and Kokoya (Bassa-Kpelle) and Gibi-Doru (Schulze 1973).

A few ethnographical surveys exist, the notable ones being those by d'Azevedo (1962, 1966, 1969, 1970, 1970-71); Johnson (1954, 1957, 1961, 1969); Holsoe (1976); Holsoe et. al. (1969); Schwab and Harley (1947); Gibbs (1963; 1960); McEvoy (1977); Fraenkel (1966); Schroder and Seibel (1974); Brooks (1972); Jones (1981); Fulton (1968); Siegmann (1969) and Gay et. al. (1969). One area where these surveyists and their linguistic collaborators have advanced much is that of classification of groups into language families. One of the most popular of these classifications is that by Schulze (1973: 50-51) who identifies five language families: West Atlantic comprising Gola and Kissi; Kru made up of Bassa, Belle, Dei, Grebo, Krahn and Kru; Mande-fu made up Gbandi, Gio, Kpelle, Loma, Mano, and Mende; Mande-tan, comprising Mandingo and Vai; and English made up of Americo-Liberians. Other classifications are to be found in Greenberg (1955, 1963); Anderson (1952) and Marinelli (1964).

These classification may have little value for analysis of ethnic conflicts because they do not provide the basis for ethnic political behaviour but they serve as linguistic summaries of otherwise complex ethnic situations (though in some cases, they could over-simplify). Another useful purpose they serve is that they sensitise us to the close family associations between ethnic groups in Liberia and those in neighbouring Sierra Leone, Guinea and Cote d'Ivoire. The Vai for example, have their kith and kin in Sierra Leone; Gola, Loma, Mano, Mandingo, Gio and Kissi in Guinea, and Grebo, Kru and Krahn in Cote d'Ivoire. Such cross-border affiliations help to explain the involvement of neighbouring countries in Liberian politics especially in the civil war.

Notwithstanding the infancy of studies of African-Liberian groups, there are a number of points that are well established about them. The first is that as already indicated, they are all small-scale and decentralised and, with the exception of the short-lived Kondo confederation at Bopolu and another organised by Zolu Doma in Vai and Gola areas, none approximated large-scale centralised political organisation. Some authors think that if the units were larger, or were welded under a dominant majority, African-Liberian would have been capable of resisting Americo-Liberian colonisation (Weiberg 1964:194). Another established point is that nearly all the groups now considered indigenous migrated to the country not too long ago. The early inhabitants are said to have migrated from the Sudan savannah following the collapse of the Sudanese empires while others came at the height of the atlantic slave trade. The Gola and Kissi are generally regarded as the earliest migrants, having moved in between 1300 and 1700, while the Grebo, Kru, Gio and Mano migrated between the 17th and 20th Centuries (Karnga 1926; Kup 1960; Johnson 1969).

An interesting case is that of the Mandingoes who came to Liberia as itinerant traders and muslim leaders from Guinea and Mauritania, at the beginning of the 19th Century. Apart from the fact that their language and culture differ from those of most other groups, Mandingoes remained itinerant and were never fully settled as Liberians until the Doe days. Anderson (1952:13) points out that up until the 1950s, Mandingo traders were regarded as foreigners and had to pay fees for licence to trade. Most indigenous Liberians regarded them as exploiters, but gradually, the Mandingoes integrated themselves using the Kondo confederation as a base and by the 1940s and 1950s, they were appointed paramount chiefs. However, 'they still remained the shrewd traders, reluctant to build houses or otherwise contribute to the permanent welfare and often the source of minor but annoying differences with the local natives' (Anderson 1952:18).

A third well known fact about African-Liberian groups is that they have cross-cutting linkages which have developed from close interaction over the years. One such linkage inheres in the fact that many African-Liberians are multilingual, with Vai, Mandingo, Kpelle and Krahn being the most widely spoken. D'Azevedo (1962) has attributed this to the early political dominance of these groups and long-standing contacts through trade, migration and shifting political alliances. The significance of multilingualism for ethnicity is that it shows the extent to which ethnic identities can be fluid and shifting depending on an individual's definition of the situation in which he finds himself. During the civil war, for example, many Gio, Mano and Krahn easily became Kpelle or Vai to avoid victimisation. Another major cross-ethnic linkage is the Poro secret society (and Sande for women) which is found in most African-Liberian groups, most notably among the Gola, Dei, Kissi, Vai, Gbandi, Kpelle and Loma. The Poro society extended from the Gola and has bound the different groups to common rituals and languages. Gay and Cole (1967:14) cite some interesting examples of how the Poro enhances inter-ethnic affiliation: 'Poro in certain Kpelle areas depend upon Gola and Loma elders to begin ceremonies. In the Gbandi tribe, the officials of Poro speak Kpelle instead of their own language'. In terms of political relevance, the Gola attempted to organise a united African-Liberian opposition to American-Liberian domination in 1918 (d'Azevedo 1969). Except for this occasion, the Poro (and Sande) societies have been organised as cultural organisations and are probably best known for the traditional 'bush school' education they give to young men and women. As part of his unification policy and in acknowledgement of the importance of the Poro in African-Liberian life, Tubman adopted it as a 'national society'.

Finally, following differences in contact and alliance with the Americo-Liberians, a gulf existed between coastal groups like the Kru and Vai who were closer to them, and the hinterland groups, many of which did not effectively become Liberian until the 1950s. In a sense, the coastal peoples saw themselves as heirs to the Americo-Liberians, and a feeling of superiority over 'up country' folks could be discerned in the attitudes of key elites of coastal origin in their relations with elites from the hinterland. This inherent tension did not lead to conflicts between the coastal and hinterland peoples as was to be expected largely because the coastal elites were marginalized under Doe. It is interesting to note, however, that most coastal peoples supported the anti-Doe struggles both before and during the civil war.

These and other inter-group linkages and uniting forces were not however sufficient to produce an indigenous Liberian counterforce to Americo-Liberian domination. One reason commonly given for this is that the indigenous ethnic groups were weighed down by internecine wars amongst themselves. Those who accept this reason however fail to see the deliberate designs of the Americo- Liberians to keep the groups apart as much as possible, and the roles they played in these wars using the instrumentality of the Liberian Frontier Force. A more important reason for the failure of the indigenous groups to respond unitedly to Americo-Liberian domination for a long time was that they were not actually Liberians until the 20th Century[10] and, even after they were integrated, they were not only excluded from the mainstream political arena, they were also denied access to eye-opening avenues like education and franchise. It took a significant number of African-Liberians to be educated and become aware of their oppression for the indigenous Liberians to respond to the domination situation.

Other Relevant Cleavages

One conclusion many studies of ethnic conflicts in Africa have made is that ethnic conflicts do not occur in pure forms because ethnic cleavages are usually recursive with regional, religious, racial and class cleavages. In other words, these other cleavages reinforce the ethnic ones and, quite often, they get so intricately interwoven that it becomes difficult to differentiate ethnic from non-ethnic conflicts. This is, for example, why regionalism in Nigeria, Cameroon and Ghana is treated as a variant of ethnicity (Osaghae 1992; Brown 1982; Levine 1976). What is the situation in Liberia? What are the other cleavages which intermesh with ethnicity and which are politically relevant?

Obviously, the first one is class which broadly followed Americo-Liberian/African-Liberian lines. The Americo-Liberian class which was the privileged class until 1980 admitted into its fold a few indigenous *evolues*, including paramount and clan chiefs who were made a part of government. The ruling class depended entirely on the state for its social reproduction and the main vocation of the Americo-Liberian was party politics and securing largesses from the government. Some of the more enterprising members of this class complemented this with being local agents and partners of foreign companies and investors like Firestone Rubber Company. Perhaps, the most remarkable characteristic of the Americo-Liberian class was that it was a leisure and lazy class. This characteristic is explained by Greenwall and wild (1936:46) thus: 'Americo-Liberians considered they had earned the right to idle in the sun. They had worked hard as slaves and now they were their own masters'. Rather than work hard on their own, 'Educated Liberians preferred to enter government, politics and law, even at lower salaries because of the

---

10   This is fully explained in Chapter 2.

economic, social, and political advantages that (followed) them' (Schulze 1973:147). Another major preoccupation of the Americo-Liberian class was freemason activity. Fraenkel (1964:192-94) traces the origins of freemasons in Liberian to the fact that the Masonic lodges were among organisations in the United States of America which financed the American colonisation society, thereby giving them a foothold from the inception of the country. The freemasons later became the main instrument of class togetherness and government, being a requirement for entry into top political appointments, including the presidency and speaker of the House of Representatives, and, of course, for recruitment and promotions in the public service. Liebenow (1969:97) records that fourteen worshipful Grand Masters of the masons included three presidents, one vice-president, chief justice, Attorney General and other top officials of state. So central Masonic activity that President Tubman once declared: '...I consider our declaration of independence to be a Masonic document and that our constitution is masonry put into political form and practice' (cited in Fraenkel 1964:193).

By 1980, following the overthrow of the Americo-Liberian/TWP oligarchy, the membership of the ruling class changed dramatically to become predominantly Africa-Liberian, though those with TWP foundations continued to hold sway. Two things distinguish the Americo-Liberian class from the post-1980 ruling class. First, the latter inherited and imitated the tendencies of the class it overthrew, a fact which preserved the 'superiority' of the Americo-Liberians. Second, the new ruling class had neither the organisational skills nor the unity of intra-class struggle along ethnic lines. Alongside this was the struggle by the Americo-Liberians to re-establish the old order. These intra- and inter-class struggles culminated in the civil war of 1989-90 which appeared to have the character of a straight-forward inter-ethnic struggle (see Chapter Five).

The non-privileged classes on the other hand were almost exclusively African-Liberian both in the pre-1980 and post-1980 eras. They comprised the urban workers (junior cadre), traders, and peasant farmers, and the vast majority of them lived in the hinterland. Relative to the privileged classes, their class consciousness was low but, as the experience of the last years of Tolbert's government and the Doe years showed, they could be mobilised effectively under harsh economic and repressive conditions as the Susukuu movement demonstrated. For a long time, the popular views were that as a political resource, ethnicity among non-privileged classes was mobilised 'only to a very limited extend because there was no participant political structure within which to mobilise it'; that 'much of the intense conflict was

15

based not on broad ethnic divisions, but on factions' (Clapham 1976:24); and that ethnicity was principally a cultural phenomenon. Developments after 1980 changed all that. Latent and incipient ethnic conflicts were galvanised into action by the new ruling class whose members had few alternative resources beside ethnicity to pursue their power interests, and the masses responded quite well, becoming ethnic champions and relating with others on this basis.[11]

Another politically relevant cleavage was regionalism defined in terms of county and other political sub-divisional identities. The fact that ethnic sub-units were the units of local administration, that ethnic groups were coterminous with counties, and that the Americo-Liberians were concentrated in the coastal countries and African-Liberian in the hinterland, made regionalism politically relevant. When, for example, Wreh (1976:45) asserts that the coastal counties — Montserrado, Cape Mount, Sinoe and Maryland — have dominated cabinet positions, he is actually referring to Americo-Liberian domination. Similarly, Krahn-Gio/Mano conflicts which dominated the Doe years also involved Grand Gedeh and Nimba counties. The point we are making is that county and other political-administrative unit identities generally reinforced ethnic identities and vice versa (Clapham 1976). However, unlike Nigeria where regional identities assumed a force entirely on their own, there could never be regionalism without the ethnic component in Liberia.

The final cleavage of relevance which is of a much more recent salience is religion. From the beginning, Liberia was defined as a Christian state and this perception, which was enshrined in the constitution, has remained popular. It however, hides the fact that the country is multireligious and that Christianity is the religion of a minority. Apart from the several christian groups -Methodist, Episcopal, Catholic, Baptist and Pentecostal and 'native' churches — there are also muslims and animists who together constitute over 70 per cent of the population. The 1964 estimates put the number of Christians at 146,000, muslims 150-250,000 and traditionalists 652-725,000 (Schulze 1973:98). Although Christians were clearly the minority, the fact that Christianity was the Americo-Liberian religion and that it was an integral part of their class character made it the dominant religion. The other religions, especially Islam, which were not given official recognition for a

---

11   As we argue in Chapters 4 and 5, Liberia's case was one of classical elite-directed ethnicity
      in which the masses were victims of false consciousness.

long time, had mainly African-Liberian adherents. Religious cleavages therefore reinforced ethnic cleavages, but it was not until the overthrow of the Americo-Liberian oligarchy in 1980 that muslims began to demand official recognition and equal treatment with christians. In fact, the civil war finally gave muslims the opportunity to assert their importance particularly because the Mandingoes who are the muslim core were major actors in the war. In 1990, Alhaji Kromah, former Director of the Liberian Broadcasting Service formed the Movement for the Redemption of Liberian Muslims which joined forces with other groups to form the United Liberian Movement for Democracy in Liberia (ULIMO).

The Nature of Ethnic Conflicts

Thus far, one point we have tried to establish is that Americo-Liberian/African-Liberian conflicts and intra-African-Liberian conflicts which became more pronounced after the 1980 coup are not, as many authors suggest two different levels of conflict. It is incorrect, for example, to see the civil war which broke out in 1989 or the several attempts to overthrow Doe as instances of conflicts among African-Liberians alone because underlying many of these conflicts were manipulations of the Americo-Liberians to return to power. So, although we can analytically differentiate between two levels of conflicts (Americo-Liberian/African-Liberian and African-Liberian/African- Liberian),[12] they cannot be separated because the domination politics of the Americo-Liberians never vanished after their overthrow.

To understand the nature of ethnic conflicts, we have to examine the objectives or stakes of ethnic competition, the organisational bases of this competition and the models of ethnic management that have existed. Let us first consider the stakes of competition. All over Africa, the major stake has been found to be control of state power which is the basis of privileges enjoyed in all spheres including employment, education, military, bureaucracy and even the private sector. It is the major source of wealth and instrument of social reproduction. In Liberia, control of the state has been even more critical because of the very weak economic base of the country. As early as 1870, the country was forced to negotiate foreign loans to

---

12   This distinction between the two levels of conflict has both analytical and practical relevance as we seek to demonstrate throughout this study. At the intra-African-Liberian level of conflict — group, subgroup and village each of which becomes important in relation to the nature of conflicts.

prevent economic collapse. All through, the country's economy, including retail trade has been controlled by foreigners — Americans and Asians mainly, and foreign aid and loans have been the life-line. In the 1970s and 1980s, global economic recession and the dwindling fortunes of rubber, iron ore, timber, and diamond — the main revenue earners in the world market, placed the country so much at the mercy of international donor agencies like the IMF that the country was practically 'up for sale'. With such weakness, government provided the only outlet to wealth and this was why, from the very beginning, the Americo-Liberians depended entirely on it to secure and preserve their privileges.

In so doing, the African-Liberians were shut out of economic privileges as even Tubman's so-called economic revolution in the open-door policy years (1944-70) did not change the concentration of wealth in the hands of only a few Americo-Liberians. This was exactly what Clower et, al. (1966:5) meant by economic growth without development: in spite of the phenomenal growth in the economy, 'the over-riding goal of Liberian authority remains what it has been...to retain political control among a small group...' Initially, conflicts between Americo-Liberians and African-Liberians were not over control of state power (see Chapter 2), but after the latter were incorporated into the country, they saw it as the only way they could hope to redress their disadvantages and enjoy the same privileges as the Americo-Liberians. As they continued to be excluded from the main arena of political participation and found opposition channels closed, they chose the option of violently overthrowing the Americo-Liberians. This overthrow did not, however, change the centrality of the state — it in fact reinforced it. For example, Clapham (1989:109) point to the instant rallying to the Doe regime by opposition forces and TWP chiefs as a reflection of the continued importance of the state as a source of power and wealth. In the Doe years, the configuration of contestants for power changed from a two-person zero-sum game situation to an n-person, n-sum game situation as more African-Liberians joined the action-set using the army (coup d'etats) and party politics. It was Doe's insistence on playing zero-sum politics in favour of his Krahn group which was clearly at variance with the new conflict situation that turned most other groups including Americo-Liberians against him.

All other narrower or micro stakes of ethnic competition — education, commerce, employment and so on are to be subsumed under the state control stake because they were all in government hands and a lot of it specifically in the hands of the President. Sawyer (1990:150) characterises the latter as the consequence of proprietary authority:

> in which a dominant leader surrounds himself with a coterie of influentials who in turn function as patrons for various sectors of the population. The public sector becomes the major instrument for the dispensing of largesse which lubricates proprietary relationships.

Proprietary authority which Sawyer traces to the colonial days, also points to the personalistic character of power and struggles for it. For one thing, personal rule has been the mainstay of power, right down to the Doe years; *all* executive appointments including those at the University of Liberia, were made by the President, and no formal distinction was made between political and non-political appointments. Much of the opposition to rulership which presents (ethnic) group forms is also highly personalised, as can be gleaned from the personal ambitions of Charles Taylor in the civil war. Here then was a classical validation of Sklar's (1967) famous thesis that ethnicity is a mask for class privilege.

Let us now turn to examine the organisational bases of ethnic conflicts. The most important have been political parties and the remarkable thing here is that the country has all along operated a one-party *de facto* system.[13] The dominant party has usually been the mainstay of the perpetuation of ethclass domination. When the mulattoes held sway, it was the Republican Party that they used, while the Americo-Liberians used the TWP to perpetuate themselves in power. In the Second Republic (1986-90), Doe hinged his power on the National Democratic Party of Liberia (NDPL) though, in truth, it was on the military. Single party dominance in a way transferred ethnic politics to the party machine as groups struggled to enhance their accesses to power through the parties. Those who preferred to form opposition parties were totally excluded from power and this explains why politicians could not afford to remain in the opposition for too long. One way the TWP managed to ward off African-Liberian opposition for a long time was to selectively admit them into the party and ensure that only those who were willing to play second fiddle climbed high. In the Second Republic, the political parties did not follow clear ethnic lines, but Doe's NDPL was Krahn and TWP remnant based.

---

13   Under this system, other parties are not disallowed from operating, but they are rendered irrelevant and incapable of competing well by the ruling party.

Another major organisational basis of ethnicity, especially on the part of African-Liberians were the ethnic unions which were based mainly in Monrovia. As elsewhere in Africa, these unions:

> owe their existence to the persistent desire for links between urban and rural tribal centres and, above all, to the new townsman's need of some form of social security and camaraderie in the alien urban milieu (Lowenkopf 1976:93).

Another major reason for their existence, which is popular all over Africa, is that they provide, through self-help efforts, the welfare needs of members which government is incapable of providing. This reason was really important in the Liberian case because the Americo-Liberian government had neither the means nor the willingness to provide these needs. By 1959, there were over 200 ethnic unions in Monrovia most of them based on ethnic sub-divisions. The activities of these groups ranged from mutual help to members in times of need (many of them were *susu* or local cooperatives) to being mobilisation agencies at election times which was the reason why some of them were formed (Fraenkel 1964). Ethnic unions also made important demands on government, as the Grand Gedeh Association which described itself as a political and mutual aid club did in 1966 when it demanded a teacher training college in Monrovia. One exceptional ethnic union was the Kru Corporation of Monrovia which was registered in 1916 as a 'property-owing body'. Its sundry activities have been described thus:

> Apart from its judicial function of settling disputes among the Kru...and the usual welfare functions, the corporation plays its most important role in connection with dockwork, the occupational interest of most Krus in Monrovia. For example, the shipping companies place a share of job assignments through the corporation. In 1958, the corporation acted as a Trade Union in a dispute with the shipping companies... (Lowenkopf 1976:91-2; also McEvoy 1977; Fraenkel 1984).[14]

In the 1970s, new variants of ethnic unions which were rural-based emerged: the traditional work societies or cooperatives (Kuus) for example. They were greatly encouraged by the Movement for Justice in Africa (MOJA) and although their main aim was to seek better marketing facilities and prices for their cash crops, they emerged as principal 'social movements which provided leadership and material support to some of the social groups that were opposed to the Liberian ruling class' (Kamara 1986:105). The

---

14   Most of these ethnic unions were organised in the areas allocated to the ethnic group, like New Kru Town and Vai Town in Monrovia.

most well known of such movements was the Susukuu which was a militant rural protest organisation established by the Putu Development Corporation of Grand Gedeh county and ably supported by MOJA. Although Susukuu was a victim of government intimidation and repression in the late 1970s, its radical opposition 'had effects far beyond Putu chiefdom, it stimulated anti-government sentiments and groups in other rural communities...' (Kamara, 1986: 105; see also Susukuu 1978; Tipoteh 1982). This way, Susukuu contributed to the popular consciousness of the 1970s that finally sounded the death knell for the Americo-Liberian/TWP hegemonic clan.

Other major organisational bases for ethnicity were popular organisations or movements, some of which brought together radical African and Americo-Liberians. There were two categories of such organisations. In the first category were those based in Liberia which were radical opposition groups most of which emerged in the 1970s to challenge Americo-Liberian/TWP oligarchic rule. These included MOJA which was led by Togba Nah Tipoteh and Amos Sawyer amongst others and PAL which was originally formed by Liberian exiles and students in the United States of America and transformed into the PPP headed by Baccus Matthews. To this category also belonged Liberian Students Union (LINSU), Students Unification Party of the University of Liberia, University of Liberia Students Union, the trade unions and the All People Freedom Alliance. These groups formed the vanguard of the popular uprisings of African-Liberians in the late 1970s, which provided the · enabling environment for the coup of 1980. These groups, especially the Student organisations continued popular opposition to Doe's dictatorial rule on behalf of the people whom Doe had lied, he came to rescue. This was in spite of Doe's strong-arm ·tactics which caused many of the members of these opposition groups to flee abroad. The second category of popular organisations comprised foreign, mainly the United States of America-based opposition groups formed by political exiles. These groups emerged after the 1980 coup and had Americo-Liberians in the dominant membership. Their major activity in the 1980s revolved around mobilising international support against the Doe government. It is instructive that Charles Taylor's NPFL had its foundation, moral and some financial support in its resolve to overthrow Doe, from these groups. One of the popular strategies adopted by these groups was to use the strong ties Americo-Liberians have with caucuses in the United States of America to further their interests in Liberia.

The final aspects of the nature of ethnic conflicts we shall consider is the models of ethnic conflict resolution or management that have been pursued in Liberia. These models have generally differed according to the phases of the country's political development. From 1847 to 1944 when Tubman initiated the unification programme, the Americo-Liberians were engaged in establishing the country and consolidating their hold on it through exclusionary strategies. With the exception of a few coastal African-Liberians who were assimilated, the coastal peoples were not regarded as Liberian citizens. Between 1944 and 1979, the orientation of the leadership was integration through incorporation of the hinterland territories. They were brought effectively under the administration of the Liberian government. Nonetheless, the coastal African-Liberians continued to be favoured such that while they got fully integrated into the county system, hinterland peoples were governed under a separate set of rules. Further, in balancing the cabinet, while hinterland African-Liberian had the privilege of ministerial appointments extended to them in the late 1950s, hinterland peoples did not until 1973 (see Table 2). The mainstay of Americo-Liberian strategy was now preservationist involving the protection of hegemonic rule and the selective incorporation of African-Liberians who could no longer be completely excluded from the power arena. The final phase — 1980-90 — the Doe years which marked the establishment of rule by African-Liberians for the first time was marked both by domination (by the Krahn) and ethnic balancing which involved attempts to make the composition of government and its major agencies representative of the ethnic interests in the country, including the Americo-Liberians. From the strategies of ethnic management we have outlined, it is clear that ethnicity in Liberia has not completely been conflictual: cooperation has also been sought particularly at the elite level.

Table 2: Ethnic Composition of Cabinets 1964-73

Ethnic Category	No. of Cabinet Ministers		
	January 1964	January 1968	May 1973
Americo-Liberian	12	12	11
Ethnic: Coastal Peoples	4	4	6
Ethnic: Hinterland Peoples	0	0	2
Total	16	16	19

Source: Clapham, 1976:48

Having analysed the nature of ethnic conflicts in Liberia, in the final section of this chapter, we formulate a model which highlights and tightens the conceptual and theoretical basis of this study. This model presents the framework according to which the analysis in the rest of the study shall be undertaken.

An Internal Colonialism Model of Analysis

In deciding on a model of analysis, the first question to be tackled is that raised by Liebenow (1987) which is whether in the light of developments since 1980 established frameworks are still valid or new ones are called for. Liebenow (1987) himself thinks that alternative approaches should be searched for. As I see it, it is not really a new approach that is required; what is required is a framework which, even if it is old conventional wisdom, can relate pre-1980 realities in logical and meaningful ways. Such an approach should be able to explain the latter as consequences of the former, and should also be able to predict future possibilities. Taking all these into consideration, I see the internal colonialism was terminated in 1980. But has the effect of that original condition come to an end? Are the unfortunate developments under Doe which led to the civil war not direct consequences of the legacy of internal colonialism? Our model assumes that they are. In fact, it would be seen that most of the so-called new perspectives, like clientelism (Clapham 1988) are actually adjuncts of this model.

· In the pre-1980 era, the major questions raised by the ethnic situation in Liberia were:

> How (did) the central elite maintain... itself and regulate ...political competition? How, and with what success (did) it involve ...the remaining people of Liberia in the political process and cope...with the problems arising from social and economic change? And how (were) the economic resources...produced and distributed to maintain the political structure? (Clapham 1978:119).

The answers are best searched for within the internal colonialism model which assumes domination by a core which is hierarchically related to a periphery. Indeed, Clapham (1978) himself uses the core-periphery categories in his analysis though he does not state explicitly that his is internal colonialist analysis. Other authors espouse a model of colonialism (Buell 1965; Liebenow 1969; 1987; Kapper et, al. 1986; Nyong'o 1987) even goes further to advance an apartheid model. Specifically, Liebenow (1987) describes the pre-1980 relationship between the Americo-Liberians and the African-Liberians as a colonial one in which the authoritative allocation of values for one group is determined by another superior group which monopolises the use of force, establishes the primary goals for all societies concerned, limits the means for these goals and attempts to determine the ultimate outcome of the relationship — continued domination, a form of integration, or eventual separation of the several societies. Here, we find Liebenow (1968) hinting at the effects of colonialism enduring beyond the colonial situation described by Balandier (see also Ekeh 1983).

Originally formulated by Hechter (1975, 1978) to explain the salience of ethnic nationalism in industrialised societies, the internal colonialism model involves a dominant core, usually a minority, and periphery which is numerically preponderant. The main assumptions of classical internal colonialism as spelt out by Birch (1978:326) are: (1) the relationship between the core and peripheral communities is based on a structured hierarchy which makes possible exploitation of the periphery by the core community; (2) the core community having acquired an advantage over the periphery in the period of state-building and/or early modernisation, uses its political and economic power to maintain its superior position; and (3) the ethnic and cultural differences between the core and periphery do not disappear and they often provide the basis for 'independence' or separatist agitations (see also Gonzates 1965; Bullivant 1984; Parkin 1974; Reece 1979; Cross 1978 and Hurstfield 1978).

These assumptions are highly applicable to the period when Americo-Liberians ruled Liberia. The response of the African-Liberians was not however separation, but a violent overthrow of that rule. Therefore, the factors making for this overthrow and why it had to be violent are integral parts of the internal colonialism model. Also, the changes in the aftermath of this overthrow and especially the responses of the former core community to the new situation are to be explained within it. What has become of the structured inequalities? Is the core community struggling to come back to its privileged position? Would the now powerful peripheral community permit this? Is internal colonialism still possible in future? Questions like these point to the centrality of competition for control of the state which, we have said, is the major object of ethnic politics in Liberia and also provides the ring of continuity for internal colonialist analysis. In other words, the struggle for state power after 1980 is best analysed as the consequence of the internal colonialist situation. A similar kind of 'consequential' analytical framework has been formulated by Mandaza (1986) for Zimbabwe — what he calls 'The Post-white Settler colonial Situation'.

2 - The Threshold of Ethnicity: A Historical Background

Up until the 1970s, Liberian history was the history of the Americo-Liberians, their settlement, establishment of the Republic, how they incorporated the other Liberians mainly through conquest, and how they held exclusively on to power at the expense of the indigenous Liberians. However, from the unification days under Tubman and in furtherance of the unification policy, historical accounts were amended to emphasise the consanguinity of American- and African-Liberians and to attribute earlier 'misunderstandings' to foreign powers, especially France and Britain (Henries 1966). Such manipulations of history cannot however wipe out the fact that the country was intended to be controlled exclusively, if possible, by the Americo-Liberians, if not ownership: the name Liberian remains a testimonial of the liberation of the settlers; Monrovia reminds them of President Monroe of the United States of America who was sympathetic to their cause; the national flag — the lone star — tells of the connection with the United States of America; the national motto: 'The love of liberty brought us here' has meaning only for the settlers; and national public holidays like Pioneers day and Matilda Newport day have little meaning for African-Liberians. One of the first demands made as soon as the 1980 coup took place was that these symbols, including the name of the country, be changed.

Of course, the African-Liberians were not passive or acquiescent subjects who willingly submitted themselves to colonial rule. From the day the first group of settlers set foot on Liberian soil, it has been a long history of Americo-Liberian conquest and domination and indigenous Liberian resistance and opposition. Two clear phases of this history can be discerned. The first is the 1820-43 phase during which the Americo-Liberians devoted themselves to state and institution-building which had them in control. At this stage, the African-Liberians were not incorporated enough to challenge the authority of the Americo-Liberians — in fact, until the 1950s, some hinterland peoples were unaware of their new identity as Liberians. The second phase 1944-90 is marked by African-Liberian challenge to the established hegemonic order which culminated in the 1980 coup. Thereafter, power struggle became a complicated n-person game, involving Americo-Liberian and African-Liberian claimants to power. The failure of Doe to expand the political arena to accommodate the enlarged participation led, in part, to the civil war which broke out in 1989. This chapter is devoted to. the first phase (1820-43) while the next will consider the consolidation of the problems in the second phase (1944-90).

Our analysis will proceed according to these two phases whose demarcations, I admit, are a little arbitrary.[15] I do not mean to suggest that there was any discontinuity between the two periods but that, in fact, the seeds of the events of the 1970s and 1980s and the built-ups towards them were sown in the first part of the country's history. By analysing the history of ethnic struggles in two phases, it should be possible to exhaustively discuss the evolution and changing character of these struggles. The objective is to properly locate the threshold of ethnic conflicts and I believe that by the time we come to the end of this chapter and the next it should be possible to see why the events of 1980 and beyond were inevitable.

1820-1944: Americo-Liberian Liberia

> The history of Liberian from its independence until world war two was one of the struggle of (the) little band of immigrants and their descendants to preserve and protect their republic. Although an estimated million or more indigenous Africans were eventually to be included within the new settlers as uncivilised savages. In fact, much of the energy of Liberia's leaders was absorbed for almost a century in a continuous struggle to subdue the recalcitrant tribes of the interior (Clifford 1971:26).

The history of how the Americo-Liberian settlers came to Liberian through the efforts of the American Colonisation Society (ACS) mainly and other colonisation societies like Maryland Colonisation Society, Mississippi Colonisation Society and Colonisation Society of the City of New York is well known.[16] The circumstances which led to the repatriation of these settlers to Africa are however worth telling for the light which they shed on their later attitudes. By 1820, there were large groups of freed slaves all over the United States of America; those freed by their Quaker masters, those freed as reward for their support in the war of independence, those freed following the abolition of slavery in Vermont 1777, other northern states in 1804, and all over the country after Congress of the United States

---

15   Most of analyses however take the Tubman era as marking a watershed in Liberian political development. Having 1944, the year of his inauguration as the beginning of the second phase may make our periodisation not so arbitrary afterall.

16   The Maryland Colonisation Society established the colony of Maryland in Africa originally as an independent colony. It joined the Commonwealth of Liberia in 1857.

of America passed a law forbidding further migration of slaves after 1808. The large number of freed slaves was considered dangerous to the American society by those who believed in protecting racial purity. One account described the freed slaves as 'persons obnoxious to the laws or dangerous to the peace of society' (Marinelli 1964:30). For reasons like these, the legislature of the State of Maryland, for example, passed a law in 1831-32 which prohibited negroes from settling in the Sate. Then, of course, there were the mulattoes. Although they were freeborn citizens, they were deprived of rights: they had no privileges of citizenship except paying tax, could not vote or be voted for or hold public office, could not marry outside their race or testify against whites in law courts.

In one word, the black community in the United States of America was an unwanted community. This fact and supposedly humanitarian considerations similar to those of colonialism being a civilising mission to Africa are said to have led to the formation in 1816 of the ACS, a voluntary private body which pioneered the Liberian project along the lines of the earlier Sierra Leone project. The ACS was officially encouraged by, amongst others, an act of Congress in 1819 which empowered President Monroe to repatriate freed slaves to Africa and to employ the United States of America navy vessels in checking activities of American slave-trading ships.

However, because of the volatile nature of the slavery issue which led to the civil war and official aversion to colonial enterprise, the United States of America government hesitated in giving open and full support to the Liberian project. In other words, 'Liberia was not a United States of America colony, and never had been one, nor was the American government willing to regard it as such. Liberia was the creation of a private philanthropic organisation ...' (Clifford 1971:21).

The negroes and mulattoes had to be persuaded to leave the United States of America as some of them expressed fears that: 'to thrust the free people of colour into the wilds of Africa without a knowledge of the arts and sciences, and without a government of any kind, is to send them into perpetual bondage' (Marinelli 1964:31). Vigorous advertising, promising opportunities and privileges which they were denied in the United States of America had to be employed to get them to agree to repatriation (Gurley 1839; Schmokel 1969). But once they agreed, a large number came to Liberia. Between 1822 when the first set of settlers landed at the mouth of river Mesurado near Monrovia and 1906 when emigration came to an end, 18, 958 negroes and mulattoes from the United States of America, West

Indies and Sierra-Leone as well as recaptured freed slaves (Congoes) were settled in Liberia.

The manner in which their settlements were acquired and enlarged by the ACS followed the classical lines of colonial acquisition in the rest of Africa, i.e. through:(1) treaties by which indigenous coastal communities acting through their chiefs either gave land to the settlers (colonisers) or acceded to their 'protection', and/or (2) conquest, which involved the subjugation of recalcitrant and hostile communities through war. The refusal of the United States of America government to officially support the project made the establishment of the 'colony' tedious, as greater reliance was on 'making book' as the indigenous communities called treaty-signing. It is very likely that if the United States of America supported the colony, displacement and possible elimination of the indigenes would have been pursued as the British did in Australia. Or they would have been confined to reservations.

The first treaty was signed in December 1821 between the ACS agents and the Dei people represented by their chiefs, and it gave the land in Cape Mesurado to the ACS (Akpan 1978; Clifford 1971). Subsequently, more treaties were signed as more settlers came. By 1830, the entire coast between Cape Mount and Grand Bassa had been acquired. Treaty-signing involved ACS agents giving cash and European goods which were erroneously assumed to be 'purchase money'. The treaties forbade the indigenous communities from further sale of land to foreign governments and brought these communities under protectorate obligations:

> to keep the paths open to traders and travellers, to abjure warfare and slave trade, and to refer inter-tribal disputes which they could not resolve amicably to the Liberian government for settlement (Akpan 1981-82:3).

Not all territories acquired through treaties, as the ACS was permanently short of funds to purchase land. In some instances, land was seized over non-payment of debts or in retaliation for attacks upon settlers. 'In short', Schmokel (1969:162) writes, 'early in Liberian history, a pattern was established in which 'Liberians' took land from the natives at will — or whenever their power was sufficient to do so'.[17]

---

17   This fact underlies the military character of the Liberian state which has persisted till this day.

The Response of the Indigenous Groups

The process of colonisation did not witness passive indigenous chiefs and their people willing to submit to the demands (or threats) of the settlers. At the initial stages, the settlers were welcomed by the coastal communities which saw them as another group of trading partners from whom they could expect benefits like payment of land rents, political-military alliances against enemy (trading) groups and Western education, especially literacy in the English language (Simpson 1961). Along these lines, Akpan (1978) attributes the initial welcome the settlers had to the high expectations which the indigenous coastal communities, through long contacts with European traders, had come to expect from association with 'civilised' people who, in this instance, better still, were black.[18] Furthermore, the indigenous communities were willing to accept the 'foreigners' for as long as they remained foreigners who would not threaten their land ownership or obstruct their trading relationships with other foreigners and especially their roles as middlemen in the trade between hinterland peoples and Europeans (a lot of this trade continued to be in slaves). Once they perceived that the settlers had come to stay and worse still, that their ACS government was bent on stopping the slave trade with the help of the United States of America navy, the coastal groups defined them as enemies and so began the famous wars which mostly were attacks on the new settlements. The first of these wars was in January 1822, followed by those of 1857, 1875, 1910, right down to the 1930s. These wars necessitated the formation of, first, the militia and later, the Liberian Frontier Force (LFF) which we discuss below.

These earliest conflicts were mostly over land, slave trade, trade with other foreigners and taxation.

On land, there was misunderstanding over the extent of ownership conferred on the settlers by the treaties. The Vai, Kru and Gola, the major coastal groups with whom these treaties were signed, had no notion of selling land — in fact, the chiefs who represented these communities had no powers to sell land. While the chiefs thought they gave land on lease to be used for trade, the colonists believed they were now owners, having paid 'purchase money'. When the settlers began to actualise this ownership,

---

18   Much earlier, French traders had been offered land to settle in as trading posts at King's Island (now Bushrod Island).

conflict became inevitable. Differences over slave trade was another source of conflict. The indigenous communities were not willing to forgo this major source of wealth. In one account given by Ephraim Bacon, ACS agent, of his negotiation with King Jack Ben at Grand Bassa, the condition given 'to make book' by the King 'was a positive stipulation... that the settlers and agents should... in no way assist the armed ships sent to the coast to suppress the 'slave trade' (Greenwall and Wild (1936:159). On the other hand, 'the colonial policy remained in adamant opposition to slave trade and to slavery, and thus to the economic interests of the coastal tribes. The immediate cause of several armed clashes was the refusal of Liberians to hand over escaped slaves', (Schmokel 1969:163). The slave trade was at issue in several wars, notably in those against the Dei in 1833, Boozie in 1839 and Kru in 1845. In these wars, the coastal groups were encouraged and supported by their European trading partners, while, from time to time, the United States of America navy supported the colonial government.[19]

Conflicts also arose from the unwillingness of the coastal trading groups to concede their lucrative middlemen role in the trade between Europeans and hinterlanders to the settlers; many of whom were engaged in trading.[20] For example, the very first clash between the colonists and Grebo at Cape Palmas occurred when the Grebo King insisted that the colonists should buy rice exclusively from him. Another source of conflict over trade was the rule by the new government that trade with foreigners could only be transacted at designated entry ports from which custom duties were collected.[21] A final source of conflicts was the refusal of indigenous peoples to pay taxes imposed on them or to succumb to forced labour.[22]

---

19   For example, Jehudi Ashmun, ACs agent, attacked Digby in 1826 and took possession of a Spanish ship, freed the slaves and forced the surrounding chiefs to sign treating forbidding slave trade in their territories. Later, with the support of the United States of America Navy, he entered parts of Grand Bassa, wiping off a place called Trade town which was a flourishing slave centre.

20   The settlers engaged mainly in export crop trade which required them to have direct dealings with the farmers.

21   The Ports of Entry Act of 1864 limited the number of coastal towns where foreigners could trade or engage in commercial activities to six. According to Vander Kraaij (1986:151), this law 'deprived the tribal people along the coast of a considerable portion of their trade'. It was repealed later by President Edwin Barclay.

22   The major tax was the hut tax. There was also the practice under which District Commissioners pawned in lieu of taxes. This practice was condemned by the League of Nations Committees, following the slavery scandal of 1923.

These conflicts did not however deter the resolve of settlers to establish their own country in which they would enjoy all the privileges they had seen whites enjoy in the United States of America and which they had been promised in the new state. Thus, most of them refused to farm because it was a mark of servitude. To further distinguish themselves from the natives (and initially, the Congoes), they referred to themselves as Americo-Liberians and consciously held on to the English language, flamboyant dressing, American-like houses, education and Christianity as the marks of their class. They challenged what was perceived to be ACS's restrictions on the maximum enjoy of their new found privileges, like not being allowed to acquire landed property and being asked to cultivate food and cash crops.

Early Government and the Beginnings of Americo-Liberian Hegemony

Americo-Liberian hegemony or, better still, their exclusive ownership of the new country was firmly put in place by the fledgling 'colonial' government which was initially headed by ACS agents or Governors as they were later called. The ACS actually drew up a constitution in 1825 which concentrated executive, legislative and judicial powers in its agent (Governor) who was all through a white until 1841 when J. J. Roberts, mulatto-settler became Governor following the death of Thomas Buchanan, the last white Governor. The constitution entitled settlers 'to all the rights and privileges of the free people of the United States of America', something which the ACS, hamstrung by financial incapability (the United States of America government constantly failed to assist it),[23] was not in a position to make good.[24] It is probable that, if there were no attacks from the natives to contend with, the settlers would have overthrown the ACS government which some of them saw as obstructing their liberty. They rioted a couple of times to protest the government's austere measures. Following one of such riots in 1824, the Rev. R. R. Gurley was commissioned by the ACS Board of Managers to write a new constitution which gave more powers to the settlers through the creation of an elected colonial advisory council which

---

23   The only significant financial help from the United States of America at the time was the US$100,000 advanced by Congress in 1819 to assist in the purchase of land, construction of homes, payment of teachers and so on.

24   In fact, the failure to have more than 19,000 settlers on the whole has been attributed to the poor finances of the ACS and other auxiliary colonisation societies (Liebenow 1969).

assisted the agent in formulating laws. The new state also went through structural changes. In 1939, it was reorganised into a self-governing commonwealth of three counties — Montserrado, Grand Bassa and Sinoe and in 1857, Maryland county founded separately by the Maryland colonisation society joined the Commonwealth. The main preoccupation of the Liberian government under the ACS, apart from attending to the needs of lazy settlers was warding off indigene attacks, acquiring more territory as more settlers came and checking slave trade. A major challenge to the new state was the hostility of British and French colonial authorities in neighbouring states and this was to force what one commentator has called a universal declaration of independence in 1847.

British colonial authority in Sierra-Leone and the French authority in Guinea and Cote d'Ivoire, as well as their trading firms refused to honour Liberian claims to coastal and hinterland territories and to pay trade duties on the grounds that a voluntary charter society could not exercise such sovereign powers. With the United States of America government refusing to be drawn into such problems, the ACS was forced to take the most viable option open to it: ask the settlers to declare Liberian a sovereign republic which they did on 26 July, 1947. This formally brought ACS 'colonisation' to an end and brought into being Americo-Liberian colonisation. Although Britain and France immediately recognised the independence of the new republic, they exploited its military and economic weakness to dispossess it of a large part of the territory to which it laid claim. This partly explains why many groups in Liberia have their kith and kin in Sierra-Leone, Guinea and Cote d'Ivoire. It should be noted that the United States of America hesitated for some time in recognising Liberian independence an even when it did in 1862, it entered into a treaty which provided, *inter alia* that the United States of America government would not 'interfere, unless solicited by the government of Liberia, in the affairs between the aboriginal inhabitants and the government of the Republic of Liberia'.[25] Another significant development that followed the declaration of independence was the necessity for the Liberian government to show its presence in the hinterland territories it claimed. This forced the government in the following years to establish a form of government over peoples who all along, never felt a part of the new order. This fact is important because it helps to

---

25   This remained a major principle of the United States of America policy towards Liberia even after Americo-Liberian rule was terminated.

explain why hinterland elites took a by far longer time than the coastal elites to get assimilated into the privileged classes.

The 1847, constitution provided for an executive presidential system of government modelled along the lines of that of the United States of America.[26] The government of Liberia was however operated only in the four coastal counties, and citizenship was restricted to negroes who owned property. It was not until 1862 that the constitution was amended to make African-Liberians subjects, not citizens, who were entitled only to civil, not political rights. The politics of the new republic was dominated by the mulatto-based Republican Party between 1847 and 1878. After then, the TWP took over and ruled for an unbroken 102 years.

The hinterland territories were not administered as part of the country until 1904 when President Arthur Barclay introduced the indirect rule system though, before then, in 1868, President James Spriggs Payne had created a Department of Interior. The introduction of the indirect rule system created a dual administration which was the hallmark of Liberian government and politics until the unification years of President Tubman. As it were, different administrative and legal codes were operated for the 'core' and 'periphery' with little or no integration between them except the President himself. An act of the legislature in 1914 limited the jurisdiction of the Liberian government to forty miles inland, and created beyond it, a vast native reserve which was placed directly under presidential rule. The hinterland 'protectorates' were not entitled to representation in the legislature. However, from the mid-1870s, an arrangement was introduced under which they could send chiefs (called 'referees') to present native problems at the legislature upon the payment of a delegate fee of US$100. These referees did not however have voting rights and, in any case, they were never more than one or two.

Before discussing the structure of indirect rule, it is important to examine the factors that necessitated it to ascertain whether, as some authors claim, indirect rule was a deliberate discriminatory contrivance which Wreh (1976:42) likens to the India reservation policy in the United States of America. The facts of the case suggest otherwise, namely, that it was a matter of necessity rather than expedience. First, the government, with the poverty it inherited from ACS, was not in a position to bear the huge costs

---

26   From the very beginning however, the legislature functioned as a subordinate and rubber stamp institution to the executive.

of administering the hinterland directly. As President Payne lamented at a point, 'shortage of funds and manpower prevented any attempt... to recognise the needs of the African tribes or to regulate their administration' (Schulze 1973:31). Moreover, even if it wanted to, the infrastructure for direct administration was just not there: in addition to manpower, there were no roads to the interior and no communication facilities. The military option was also not viable, as President Barclay himself admitted:

> the Americo-Liberian elements cannot control the enormous native population by military force. There is not enough of it... Therefore, we must trust and use the civilised native Liberian to manage his own people, or to assist us the Americo-Liberians in doing so (Akpan 1986:124).

Finally, indirect rule provided a cheap and less troublesome method for the President and Americo-Liberians to keep the African-Liberians in check. For one thing, indirect rule kept the groups apart and, for as long as the President had the power to approve the authority of local chiefs, the situation could always be manipulated to ensure loyalty.

Under the indirect rule system, the hinterland was divided into three provinces, Eastern, Western and Central (while the coastal territories were governed according to the county system). Each province was further divided into districts which, in turn, were subdivided into paramount chiefdoms. The basic unit of administration was the paramount chiefdom which consisted of between thirty-four and sixty villages of the same or different ethnic group(s). Each paramount chiefdom was headed by a paramount chief elected by clan and town chiefs (who were themselves elected) and approved by the President. Paramount chiefs were directly under the District Commissioner (DC) who was the President's representative and also the commander of the LFF unit in the district.[27] Being far from Monrovia, and with no communication facilities, DCs were quite powerful, corrupt and oppressive (Akpan 1982-83:143). Paramount chiefs were indirect agents of the President. Their major duties included performing traditional functions which included heading 'tribal courts', collecting taxes, levies and annual tribute of rice,[28] and labour recruitment (for porterage, road construction and other works). For a long time,

---

27 This fact further reinforced the military nature of internal colonialism.
28 The chiefs were not paid salaries, but were entitled to 10 per cent of all taxes and levies collected.

34

paramount chiefs, who were required to meet certain minimum standards of 'civilisation' remained the most notable hinterland elements in government.

Strategies of Control

Apart from the indirect rule system, the strategies employed by the Americo-Liberians to subdue the African-Liberians and consolidate their hold on power included the coercive instruments of the LFF (later Liberian National Guard), restrictions on educational facilities and the patronage system of the TWP. These strategies were in existence up to the 1970s, and it is interesting to know that their foundations lay quite early in the country's history, which further reinforces the argument that the Americo-Liberians from the very beginning wanted a country entirely their own if possible. We shall discuss these strategies briefly in turn.

LFF

Hostility towards the settlers and the incessant attacks on them necessitated the establishment of a military force. Akpan (1986:23) has dealt at great length with the precedents of military organisation which also determined the role of the military in the colonisation period and beyond. The most fundamental of these was that:

> Liberia needed both a strong military force and its constant display or use to keep the indigenous Liberians submissive to Liberian government authority and deter them from aggression against the Americo-Liberians... (Akpan 1986:123).

In other words, military conquest was expected to play a crucial part in the colonisation process, a fact which made the Liberian state, like most other colonial states, a military state. This was the background against which the constitutions of 1825, 1839 and 1847 provided for the organisation of a militia force, and gave a right for the people (Americo-Liberians) to bear arms in their common defence. The President, as commander-in-chief, had the power to mobilise the militia for the purpose of war, implying that, from the beginning, the anglo-saxon principle of civilian control of the military was established (it was broken only in 1980). The militia force which began as a volunteer and later compulsory service for able-bodied men aged between 15 and 50 gradually grew in number and organisational complexity, as Congoes and apprentice-indigenes, as well as recruits from 'warrior tribes' (Kpelle, Loma and Gbandi especially) joined the force. In 1865, it had about 1200 enlisted men, though, it remained a non-standing army whose main function was defence against attack when called upon to do so.

The military needs of Liberia changed after 1884-85 when, harassed by the British and French, it was forced to effectively occupy the territories it laid claims to. It became necessary to establish a standing army capable of conquering any recalcitrant group resisting Liberian authority. This was the situation under which the LFF came into being in 1908. The force was placed initially under the command of a British officer, Major M. Cadell but was later put under American command as part of an aid programme after a plot by Major Cadell to overthrow the government was uncovered. With a weak economic base, the country was never able to organise a large or strong army and relied greatly on indigenous allies to propagate its wars.[29] Nonetheless, the LFF was a brutal army of occupation in the hinterland districts. It was particularly notorious for dehumanising African-Liberians and the Charity and Brunot Commissions set up to investigate the Liberian administration by the League of Nations called for a reorganisation of this force.[30] One interesting thing to note about the LFF which became the National Guard and later the Liberian army is that although its officer corps was Americo-Liberian for a long time, it was the only institution that admitted African-Liberians with little restriction. As the access was closed to them in most other spheres, it was not surprising that the overthrow of the Americo-Liberian oligarchy was effected by African-Liberian soldiers of non-commissioned ranks.

Education

One institution which reinforced and sustained the class distinctions between the settlers and indigenes from the beginning, was education. Although, it was supposed to be part of the 'civilising mission', as hoped by the ACS, the Americo-Liberians who were themselves not well educated saw it as a way of maintaining their superiority over the African-Liberians and of keeping them in servitude. Here, a difference in perception could be observed between the ACS Governors and the Americo-Liberians. Jehudi Ashmun, (ACS Governor), for example, believed education of Africans was

---

29   This was one way in which the Liberian authorities were able to sustain the policy of divide and rule.
30   The investigation followed allegations of slavery levelled against the Liberian authorities.

a major goal in the colonisation project, and hoped that through Christianity, the English language and education, the natives could become 'perfectly identical' to the Americo-Liberians. Other agents and Governors felt the same way and therefore included provision of education in several treaties with indigenous groups. Some of them opposed the Americo-Liberian scheme of selective education which involved what Schmokel (1969:166) describes as assimilation through 'temporary slavery': the practice whereby native parents bound their children to settler families as apprentices or pawns until they reached maturity.

But educational facilities, including Liberia College which was founded in 1861 were restricted to the counties and to the Americo-Liberians (including Congoes) mainly.[31] Even if the Liberian government wanted to expand the facilities which it was not willing to do, it lacked the financial resources to do so. In fact, most schools were missionary schools (in 1922, there were only 46 government schools compare to 128 missionary schools). Knowing its handicap, government made the establishment of an elementary school at least, a condition for approving missionary activity in coastal communities.

However, it clamped down on missions that encouraged native integrity and assertiveness. For example, the activities of the episcopal mission were restricted in Maryland county where it was accused of encouraging Grebo revolts. The methodists who encouraged the development of vernacular languages were viewed with suspicion. Indeed, until the 1940s, missions were not permitted to establish churches and schools more than 50 miles into the interior, except on special grounds. For example, 'christian mission stations at Bolahun, Ganta and other points far into the interior were established, not to encourage Christian missionaries, but rather as bulwarks against the south-ward penetration of Mandingo and other Muslim influences extending southward into (Monrovia)' (Liebenow 1987:53-54).

The major reason why access to education by the hinterland and coastal African-Liberians was restricted was the valid fear that they could easily outnumber the Americo-Liberians whose basis for a claim to superiority was education. In other words, making education available to the numerically preponderant natives was tantamount to committing a class suicide'. 'Ignorance is bliss' was the ground for denying African-Liberians education (Hayman and Preece, 1943). The few of them who got good education did so as apprentices, adopted children or by simply adopting

---

31   Thus, in its first sixty years of existence, Liberia College produced only seventy graduates.

Americo-Liberian names. As the Americo-Liberians feared the increased number of educated African-Liberians became the bastion of challenge to their exclusive privileges in later years.

TWP

As the single-party *de facto*, the TWP was the major instrument of Americo-Liberian hegemony all through. The party controlled power for an unbroken period of 102 years during which its standard-bearers — as Presidential candidates are known, chairman and other top party functionaries were Americo-Liberian. As African-Liberians, beginning with the coastal peoples, got integrated into the Liberian state, so were their elites admitted into the TWP, making it, not a closed, but a cadre party (Lowenkopf 1971:123) or, as Clapham (1976:53) says, the party of the 'governing elite'. But as we emphasised in chapter one, the African-Liberian elite in the TWP was admitted as a comprador, and no room was given for the creation of independent power bases. The real power of the TWP, for both the Americo-Liberian and African-Liberian lay in its being the President's instrument for determining who got what, when and how, in the patronage system. In addition to deciding who would run for which election and appointing people to his cabinet and other top government positions, the President was in charge of employing people (including junior officers) in government, granting commercial licences and cash subventions, and approval of land purchases. In short, as Buell (1965:712) observed, 'Every officer in the government, whether a judge or administrator, must belong to the True Whig Party before he can secure appointment'. As the main instrument for determining access to state power, the Americo-Liberian politicians, using the justification of the dual administrative set-up excluded hinterland Liberians from membership for a long time, and even after they were fully integrated into the county system in the 1960s, the franchise continued to be restricted to prevent native take-over. Within the party itself, African-Liberian politicians like Didwho Twe who dared to challenge the standard-bearers were put in their 'proper' places (see Chapter 3).

These, in brief, were the main strategies by which the Americo-Liberians established and sustained their hegemonic rule at the early stages. They underwent sophistication and increased systematisation as African-Liberian challenge to this rule gathered momentum in later years. Perhaps the greatest drawback to the Americo-Liberian designs and the major factor which made control of the state and connection with government the critical objects of ethnic and class (and, of course, intra-ethnic and intra-class) competition was the poverty and economic weakness of the county. This problem which has been constant in Liberian politics has its roots in the country's early history. This is the issue we shall consider next.

Economic Weakness of the Liberian State: Its Roots

We have hinted at the economic weakness of the Liberian state, beginning from the financial insolvency of the ACS and American unwillingness to help, and the necessity for indirect rule. The situation became really desperate a few years into independence when wars with hinterland groups and the underdevelopment of infrastructure prevented capacity utilisation of hinterland resources; the major export crops — coffee, sugar cane, indigo and oil palm faced still competition in the world market, and foreign traders refused to pay duties on goods. Faced with the threat of collapse, a Liberian delegation was sent to London to negotiate for private loan in 1870. The mission was unsuccessfully because Liberia was adjudged not credit worthy. However, in 1871, foreign loans totalling £100,000 were successfully negotiated and secured, only to be misappropriated by President E. J. Roye.[32] Then in 1909, following entreaties to the United States of America government to advise on internal affairs, establish a bank in Liberia, exploit her resources and persuade European commercial concerns to be liberal with her, the United States of America state department set up a commission of enquiry to investigate the country's economy. The commission found financial impropriety of government officials rampant and that 'an empty treasury is so frequent as to be almost the rule'. In the aftermath of this investigation, the United States of America instituted another commission to manage Liberian economy which was sufficient guarantee for another loan of £340,000 from a consortium of United States of America, English, French, and German banks. The security for this loan was revenue from customs, which was the major source of income.[33]

At this stage, control of the Liberian economy had passed on to the club of international capitalists led by the United States of America. Part of the implications of this was that the ruling class could no longer have an independent material base, a fact which has historically made it a classical

---

32 Roye later drowned while attempting to make away with his loot.
33 In the 1980s, after a period of boom from rubber and iron ore, Liberia returned, once again, to this situation.

39

comprador. The immediate effect of the dependence on loans, however, was the exposure of the country to foreign control. For example, it was forced to abandon a policy of neutrality during the First World War when the allied countries withdrew their credit line on account of its continued trade with Germany. Twice in 1893 and 1908, because of economic problems and threats from British and French creditors, the Liberian government was practically begging the United States of America government to be colonised. The introduction of austerity measures following the global economic recession of the post-War era could not salvage the economy, as the country found it extremely difficult to secure more loans.

The life-line came in 1926 when Firestone Rubber Company of the United States of America was granted free lease to exploit Liberia's rubber resources. For a long time, afterwards, in fact, up until the 1960s, Firestone virtually controlled the Liberian economy. Two instances of this control can be cited: in 1926, it arranged a US$5 million syndicated loan to facilitate large-scale investment; and after the British Bank of West Africa closed down its operations in Monrovia, a Firestone subsidiary, took over, and provided banking services for over 20 years. Moreover, in its agreement with Firestone, the Liberian government practically 'sold-off' the country's sovereignty, something which Simpson (1961) has defended on the grounds of eliciting greater American attention.[34] Of course, the entry of Firestone created new vistas for the Americo-Liberians who were desperate to ground their hegemony on an 'internal' material base.

How did these characteristics of the economy affect ethnic relations? First, although the bulk of economic activities took place in Monrovia, the Liberian government stepped up its claims over the hinterland where the cash crops and other resources were. Second, because there was too little to go around and because that little was in the hands of government, the Americo-Liberians tightened their control on it. In later years, the same situation of economic scarcity would heighten African-Liberian challenge of Americo-Liberian domination. Third, the entry of Firestone and the subsequent pull of rural labour into the 'modern' economy facilitated the economic integration of the counties and provinces, and afforded several hinterland peoples, the opportunity to feel, for the first time, that they now belonged to a new country. Finally, the exposed and dependent nature of the

---

34 Again, this strategy of calling for American attention was a dominant theme in the 1980s under Doe.

40

national economy meant that external forces would always play a part in conflicts of a purely local nature. Most of these effects have remained till today.

The 1928 Scandal

No consideration of the threshold of ethnicity in Liberia can ever be complete, without a look at the slave trade scandal which led the League of Nations (hereafter the 'League') to institute an investigation into the affairs of the country. The outcome of that investigation aptly summarises the directions of Americo-Liberian/African-Liberian conflicts in the foundation years. The fact of the case was that in 1928, allegations were brought to the League that Americo-Liberians, including top government officials were selling indigenous Liberians into slavery at Fernando Po.[35] The Charity Commission which the League set up to investigate the matter indicted many top government officials, including the Vice President over the matter, and criticised the method of governing the indigenous peoples. The Commission went on to make recommendations which were to the effect that African-Liberians should be accepted as citizens: (1) that barriers to the full assimilation of the natives should be removed; (2) educational opportunities should be expanded and made equal; (3) the pawnage system should be stopped; (4) the LFF should stop intimidating hinterland peoples; and (5) Liberian doors should be opened to foreign investment. The significance of these recommendations was that the Americo-Liberians had to integrate the African-Liberians into the new state as equals. The pressures were enormous. The United States of America threatened to 'alienate all friendly feelings' if the policy of suppressing natives was not stopped. Britain and France championed a campaign that Liberian was incapable of governing itself and should therefore be placed under a governing commission of the League — in fact, a book published in 1929 urged a replacement of the negro government in Liberian by 'strong, high-minded whitemen' (Simon 1922).

The Liberian government could not afford to discountenance these pressures particularly because of its dependent economy. The immediate response was the acceptance of the recommendations of the League.

---

35 This allegation is believed to have been orchestrated internationally by Thomas Faulkner who lost the Presidential election to King in the 1920s.

Pawning was outlawed, the hinterland was declared open to foreign investors, the barriers to assimilation were 'abolished', and the United States of America was asked to nominate two commissioners to supervise administrative reforms in the administration of the hinterland. This was the background to the unification and open-door economic policies which were launched by President Tubman at his first inauguration in 1944. But was the equality principle acceptable?

Clearly, ethnic conflicts in Liberia began as a matter of Americo-Liberian/African-Liberian conflicts. The African-Liberians of reference were actually the coastal peoples who attempted to preserve their autonomy against the settlers. The hinterland peoples were, for all practical purposes not part of the country; they constituted a 'reserve' from which resources, including slaves were to be procured, as the League Commission found out. Furthermore, while hinterland peoples were governed indirectly, coastal peoples were governed directly as they were made a part of the county administration. In fact, under a naturalisation system, coastal peoples could acquire citizenship status through a three year period of apprenticeship and abandonment of 'savage' ways.[36] This did not mean that they were equal to the Americo-Liberians or that they were really better off than their hinterland counterparts in material terms. But the coastal- hinterland distinctions among African-Liberians are important because, they explain, in part, why the Americo-Liberians were able to sustain their hegemonic rule for as long as they did. By selectively admitting the coastal peoples, the Americo-Liberians built a class of people who did not feel as deprived as the hinterland peoples even after the effective integration of the latter. This prevented a unity of coastal and hinterland African-Liberian groups. This unity would have most likely brought about the overthrow of the *ancien regime* earlier than 1980.[37] It took the incorporation of the hinterland peoples and their resentment of being made second-class citizens for the coastal peoples to begin to realise that they were not really part of the Americo-Liberian group. How this happened and the circumstances that forced this unity will, hopefully, be made clear in Chapter 3.

---

36   This way, members of the Sinoe group were admitted into citizenship upon petition, and this was later extended to other groups in the coastal counties.

37   This issue is fully discussed in Chapters 4 and 5.

3 - Consolidating Hegemonic Rule and the Seeds of Destruction Within

Although doubts have been expressed over the appropriateness of describing a peripheralised ruling class which lacks an independent material base and which is consistently challenged from within as a hegemonic class (Ihonvbere and Falola 1984), no better or more appropriate description can be found for Americo-Liberian rule in Liberia after the state-building process was consolidated. Hegemony has been defined as:

> an order in which a certain way of life and thought is dominant, in which one concept of reality is diffused throughout society in all its institutions and private manifestation informing with its spirit all tastes, morality, customs, religions and political principles and all social relations, particularly in their intellectual and moral connotations (Williams 1960:587).

Nothing in this definition requires that, for a hegemonic class to exist, it must not be challenged by other classes or that it must be materially autonomous. What makes it a hegemonic class is the fact that it is able to control the other groups, check challenges to its supremacy and perpetuate this order. Gramsci (1971) says this process can be carried on through (1) control over coercive instruments of state (class domination), and (2) moral and intellectual leadership through which the class imposes its will on society without having to use force. The Americo-Liberians certainly had such controls.

The point, however, is that hegemonic rule may persist but it does not last for ever. The dominated group challenges it to the point when it is able to overthrow it. The circumstances which result in this eventual overthrow are provided, willy-nilly, by the hegemonic class itself. In the case of Liberia, beginning from 1944, the Americo-Liberians were willing to integrate African-Liberians as citizens, but were not willing to accord them the privileges of this status nor to expand the access to political power to accommodate the 'new Liberians'. As integration progressed, so did African-Liberians realise that they could not remain perpetually in servitude. This was how the hegemonic rule of the Americo-Liberians sowed the seeds of its own destruction. This Chapter, which is a follow-up to the last one in the manner of a historical aftermath examines how, even with 'unification', Americo-Liberian hegemony was consolidated, and how this process produced the revolutionary spirit among the African-Liberians. As we specified in Chapter 2. This Chapter is devoted to the period 1944-1980.

Any analysis of Liberian politics within the period (1944-80) cannot but be an analysis of the Tubman years (1944-1972) which are the most any President has ever had in Liberian history and which set the course for the Tolbert years which followed. While many students of Liberian history positively appraise his unification and open door policies as marking major advances in the country's political development others, like Wreh (1976), accuse him of not going far enough, of not being sincere and of being a tyrant. Similar differences attend the appraisal of President William R. Tolbert (1972-1980) under whom the established order was finally overthrown. Our concern is not, however, to assess the performances of these Presidents *per se*; it is to see how these performances impacted upon ethnic relations in the country. Was there a genuine intention to integrate the African-Liberians, not only administratively but also structurally into the power matrix? Or was it a case of passing crumbs from the Americo-Liberians table? What were the reactions of the African-Liberians and of Americo-Liberians? Did policies under Tubman and Tolbert continue to emphasise these cleavages? These are some of the questions which guide the analysis under the headings which follow.

The Unification Policy

In the period 1820-1944, as we saw in Chapter 2, Liberia was governed as two countries rather than one, and not even the intervention of the League could make the government put an end to this duality. But the implication of the League's recommendations could not be lost on subsequent governments, and the 'commitment' to unification in the Tubman-Tolbert years, can, in part, be attributed to this. At his first inauguration in 1944, Tubman launched a unification policy which aimed at the 'assimilation and unification of our various populations'. In pursuit of this policy, which became the hallmark of his administration, important changes which aimed at greater incorporation of African-Liberians, especially those of the hinterland, were effected. The most prominent changes included: (1) reforms of hinterland administration which saw the removal of unpopular District Commissioners and the appointment of provincial commissioners to implement these reforms. This process was completed in 1964 with the dismantling of the provincial administrative structure and its replacement with the country system, thus ending the dual administrative structure in the country; (2) the opening up of the hinterland areas through road and other infrastructural development, and the expansion of educational facilities; (3) amendments to the 1847 constitution to increase the political rights of hinterland African-Liberians; the franchise was extended to them, though it was restricted to those who paid hut tax; they were given legislative representation for the first time though, again, care was taken not to let their representatives dominate the Senate and House of Representatives; and they were granted permission to carry arms; and (4) the number of African-Liberians in government positions including the cabinet increased tremendously, though the bulk continued to be given to the coastal groups — hinterlanders were not appointed to ministerial positions until the early 1970s (see Table 2 in Chapter 1).

For Tubman, unification meant familiarising with and endearing himself to the African-Liberians. He visited several hinterland territories and also held cabinet meetings from time to time in hinterland towns, a practice which Tolbert continued. He set up National Unification Councils to which he appointed all paramount and clan chiefs and elders from villages, to review the unification programme periodically. At the inaugural meeting of this body in 1954, Tubman reiterated his desire to melt existing cleavages:

> we must now destroy all ideologies that tend to divide us. Americo-Liberians must be forgotten, and all of us register a new era of justice, equality, fair dealing and equal opportunities for everyone from every part of the country regardless of tribe, clan, section, element, creed or economic status (Townsend 1959:236).

How genuine were these declarations? The unification programme recorded some notable successes and certainly brought hinterland African-Liberians effectively into Liberia, but this had to be done in a way that would not threaten Americo-Liberian/TWP hegemony. In fact, it has been suggested that the unification programme was introduced to prevent the rise of nationalist agitation by the African-Liberians, as this period marked the height of nationalist activities in Africa (Lowenkopf 1976).

Within the context of Americo-Liberian hegemony, the unification programme could also be explained as part of Tubman's strategy to sustain himself in power. Tubman realised the threat posed by continued exclusion of African-Liberians from power, not only to the Americo-Liberians, but also to himself. He also hoped to create a new power base which could rescue him from total dependence on the Americo-Liberians who, in the past, brought down Presidents who were not ready to 'play ball'.[38] But, at

---

38   Presidents were held to ransom in the past by powerful politicians. Anthony Gardiner (1878-1883) had to resign under conditions of opposition, and Charles D.B. King (1920-1930) was actually forced to resign.

the same time, he could not lose sight of the numerical power of the African-Liberians which, if they were given full political rights, could have been used to wrest power from the minority Americo-Liberians. This explains why integration was not attended by any dramatic expansion of political participation. One strategy Tubman employed to further check the threat of African-Liberians becoming too powerful for comfort was to ensure that no ethnic group or politician enjoyed special treatment:

> ...Just as he sought to maintain a balance among the older elite and to dilute their power by recruiting new members into government, he sought to deny to any one tribal group a special position vis-à-vis the others, or a position of great influence within the government. Many Krus, Vais and Grebos held high office under Tubman and at times, one or another of these groups was considered to be in the political ascendancy. But if a tribal leader sought to construct an independent base of power within his tribe, Tubman quick to (deal with) him (Lowenkopf 1976:5-6).

Then, there was the economic necessity for unification, namely, that it provided the basis for the success of the open-door policy which we shall discuss shortly. With unification, the hinterland was opened up for exploitation by foreign investors. The prosperity from this exploitation did not go to the African-Liberians; it was used to strengthen the (dependent) material basis of the hegemonic class.

The unification policy nevertheless, recorded some successes that benefited African-Liberians (of the hinterland especially). In terms of road construction and other infrastructural development, the progress was remarkable. From a situation in 1945 where there was no single paved or hard-surfaced road in the whole of Liberia, there came the 1969 situation where there were 3000 miles of paved and surfaced roads, 70 per cent of which were in hinterland territories. Educational facilities were expanded and the African-Liberians made progress which was to 'open their eyes' to their servitude in later years.[39] By 1973, there were about 153,000 children in elementary school all over the country of which more than two-thirds were African-Liberians, though again, the bulk was from coastal communities. We have already talked about the enfranchisement of hinterland Liberians and the right they were granted to elect representatives in the legislature, as well as the appointments of African-Liberians to top government positions, including ministerial and ambassadorial positions. By 1963, four of the sixteen-man cabinet were African-Liberians and another

---

39   The slogan of the 'upcountry' folks after the 1980 coup was 'our eyes are now open'!

two were of mixed parentage. By 1973, two of the three Generals on the active list of the Liberian army were Loma, and another half of the officer corps was made up of African-Liberians (part of the reason for this was the low prestige ranking of being in the army). Giant strides were also recorded in the cultural sphere which, in part met the needs of a de-rooted hegemonic class seeking to establish a national culture. Official recognition was granted to Poro and Sande societies which Tubman called the symbols of national cultural revival. He organised a 'national' Poro society, thereby bringing under government control an institution he perceived could be used by the African-Liberian to launch a united front. A Bureau of Folkways was created and, in 1963, a National Cultural Centre was built in Monrovia with 16 huts representing the 16 major ethnic groups. The 1847 Declaration of Independence was also translated into Vai and other languages. The national cultural revival was so vigorously pursued that some coastal African-Liberian politicians who had earlier changed their names to anglo-saxon names to be assimilated reverted to their old names.

On balance, however, the unification scheme failed to elevate the status of African-Liberians in any dramatic way for reasons which were outlined earlier on. The old order remained essentially. A dual legal code continued to exist, as hinterland peoples were governed by 'tribal laws' in so far as these did not conflict with the statutory laws. To prevent African-Liberians from the coastland and hinterland from joining forces, a policy which Liebenow (1969:55) has likened to the land reserve policy of British settlers in East Africa and whites in South Africa was operated under which areas of land were allocated separately to ethnic groups in Monrovia. In other areas:

> A member of the group [had] a right to land in his tribal area, but a tribal stranger [could] take up residence only with the permission of the traditional leadership and upon the stranger's acceptance of the local chief's political authority.

Other examples of anti-African-Liberian policies and continuities can be cited. Tubman encouraged more immigrations from the United States of America and the West Indies which he called 'new blood to our own race' with a view to forestalling the Americo-Liberian minority group from being eaten up. For all of the seven terms he served, he never considered any African-Liberian politician qualified to be made vice-president, a policy which Tolbert continued. Then, of course, there was the retention of national symbols which all reflected Americo-Liberian hegemony.[40] For these and other reasons, Lowenkopf's (1976:3-4) conclusion that unification did not shake the foundations of basic cleavages is valid:

> Most tribal people still did not have access to the citadels of political and economic power, or easy and open association with the ruling elite... Deep and persistent differences in culture and values continued to separate tribal Liberians from the descendants of Americo-Liberians.

Chaudhuri (1986:47) is even more emphatic: 'Despite the introduction of some liberal measures to broaden the base of the administration by... Tubman, real power continued to be in the hands of an oligarchy'. In spite of his failings, many hinterland African-Liberians considered Tubman far more sympathetic to their cause than Tolbert was. While it is true that Tolbert was not as forthcoming on unification as Tubman was, he did not abandon the policy. For example, he created a Commission on National Unity, headed by McKinley A. De-Shield, to examine state and official documents which functioned to divisive ends and recommend appropriate measures. He continued with the practice of holding executive meetings in hinterland counties and went further than Tubman in appointing hinterlanders to government positions. In 1976, Tolbert even promised to change the country's constitution, anthem, motto and flag saying, 'they no longer correctly and appropriately reflected Liberia's African heritage' (West Africa 1976:1789). But these did not impress the people. To them, Tolbert was a typical Americo-Liberian champion who believed that the natives were not qualified for an extension of political power. It is significant that President Samuel Doe constantly resurrected the spirit of Tubman in his calls for national unity — in fact, Tubman was made father of the nation whose birthday was observed as a national holiday.

The Open Door Policy

From the beginning, as we saw in Chapter 2, the Liberian economy was very poor and almost completely dependent on foreign loans and aid. The coming of Firestone in 1926 seemed to indicate that perhaps the solution to the crisis was to throw the doors open to foreign investors since Liberia lacked the financial, technical and manpower resources to undertake the

---

40 Organized groups which championed the cause of African-Liberians begun to demand changes. In 1972, University of Liberia students demanded a change in the national motto to reflect the fact that the country no longer belonged to the Americo-Liberians alone.

48

exploitation itself. Contrary to what Marinelli (1964) suggests, the open-door policy was not initiated to provide equal economic opportunities for the African-Liberians. It was introduced to strengthen the country's economic base and at the same time, to bolster the economic base of the Americo-Liberian hegemonic class through greater agreement and, well defined compradorisation with foreign investors.[41] Foreign investors were 'to bring in capital and to remit profits, dividends and other earnings without interference or impediments...' (Clifford 1971:103-4). These superfluous terms attracted several foreign commercial interests: Liberia Mining Company (United States of America-based), Bong Mining Company (German-based), International African-American Corporation (United States of America-based) and the Liberian-American-Swedish Mining Company (LAMCO), etc. While these Companies mined iron-ore, Firestone monopolised rubber, and with the two main export commodities under foreign control, open-door simply meant consolidating a situation which all along was ad hoc. Apart from increased foreign control of the domestic economy, foreign loans remained the backbone of the economy. The Free Port of Monrovia was built with a grant of US$22 million advanced by the United States of America for Liberian support for the allied forces during the Second World War, while under the Point 4 technical assistance programme in 1949, a joint United States of America-Liberia Commission for Economic Development was established. This Commission negotiated several short and long-term loans, part of which enabled the government to repay the US$5 million Firestone loan of 1926, in 1952. Debt servicing between 1964 and 1970, accounts for 20-25 per cent of the national revenue.

Statistically, the benefits of the open-door policy were impressive. Total foreign investment in Liberia had increased from US$3 million in the 1940s to over US$1 billion in 1970 (Clower et. al. 1966; Beleky 1973) and in the 1950s, Liberia enjoyed the highest percentage increase in per capita GNP in the world! But, as the economic survey carried out by Clower et. al. (1966) found, it was a classical case of growth without development. There was the

---

41   It is generally known that the African bourgeoisie lacks a material base and is essentially dependent on the international capitalist class. This is even more pronounced in the Liberian situation and, the point being made here, is that the open door policy afforded the opportunity for streamlining the dependency links. Nonetheless, there were criticisms by patriotic elements of the ruling class who saw in open door policy an invitation to a new form of colonial domination.

fact that Liberians had very limited part in the ownership of their own economy. For instance, of the about US$382 million invested in the iron-ore sector in 1962, only about US$8.5 million belonged to Liberians. With open-door also came increased consumption of foreign goods and food, as well as the incorporation of hinterland Liberian into the world capitalist system as an object of exploitation. It is true that opportunities were created in the plantations and mining companies for Liberians (Americo and African) for employment, but the African-Liberian could not make good use of them because they did not possess the necessary educational and technical skills. Consequently, they were employed mainly as labourers, unskilled workers, artisans and clerks.[42] This brings us to the main impact the open-door policy: it helped to bolster the economic base of the Americo-Liberians whom Clower et. al. (1966) have shown were the major beneficiaries of the 'boom'.[43]

The boom brought about by the open door policy did not last because it was contingent upon iron ore and rubber — the main export commodities with favourable world market. In the 1970s, they fared very badly, forcing some of the foreign companies to close down production. Of course, the effect was another period of economic hardship. Tolbert's attempts to build a self-reliant, inward-looking economy and the introduction of austerity measures in the late 1970s, proved to be quite costly for him and the oligarchy, as we shall find out in the final part of this chapter.

Personal Rule

One feature of governance in Liberia from inception which Tubman transformed into an art, and carried on passionately by Tolbert, was personal or authoritarian rule. Personal rule refers to a situation where it is difficult to differentiate the ruler from the government, and is often the product of the neutralisation of institutional checks by the legislature and judiciary. Even elections become mere routine exercises as opposition is

---

42 The foreign companies had the bulk of its junior work force recruited from the groups in the places where they were located; the Kpelle dominated the work force in Firestone's largest plantation at Harbel, followed by the Kissi, Bassa, Loma and Gio, all proximate groups, while the smaller plantation at Cavalla had a preponderance of Grebo and Kru. Similarly, the work force of LAMCO in the Nimba range was predominantly Mano and Gio.

43 This was because neither structural nor institutional changes in the area of income distribution, for example, accompanied the growth process.

discountenanced.[44] The strategies of personal rule include use of coercive instruments, including draconian laws to repress the civil society and opposition movements, the reduction to irrelevance of opposition parties where they are allowed, the centralisation of the patronage system around the ruler and his exclusive use of it to reward loyalists, punish opponents and manipulate support constituencies and the emphasis on family, kin and other nepotic ties in appointments to government positions (Decalo 1989). Along these lines, most Liberian leaders have operated personal authoritarian rulerships, and this was one legacy which the government of Samuel Doe inherited. The immediate result of personal rulership was a decay of political institutions, but in the long run, it was personal rule that sustained Americo-Liberian hegemony for a long time. If government was de-personalised, and institutions were allowed to function properly, it would have been difficult to exclude African-Liberians from the power process. In a similar vein, Krahn domination would have been impossible under Doe's civilian administration if the legislature, press and the judiciary were not rendered redundant and if the rules of rational bureaucracy were allowed to operate.

Both Tubman and Tolbert, whom we are immediately concerned with, were personal authoritarian rulers *par excellence*. Tubman, for one, made great use of fraternal and secret societies which provided one of the most formidable institutional bases for Americo-Liberian hegemony, as membership was restricted to them.[45] Tubman belonged to all the fraternal orders (including the indigenous Poro society) and this made him the Grand Master of Masons of Liberia. Family ties were also very important and, in practice, Americo-Liberian hegemony amounted to the hegemony of only a few families associated through marriages: the most notable families were the Barclays, Grimeses, Dennis', Weeks, Tubmans, and Tolberts. These families enjoyed the plums and select privileges and under Tolbert, the greatest beneficiaries were members of his immediate family — his elder brother, Frank, was President *pro tempore* of senate, while his younger brother was Finance Minister until his death in 1975.

44　Elections have never been a good side of Liberian politics. They are usually predictable, as it is abnormal for an incumbent to lose. The Guiness Book of Records also gives to Liberia, the record of 'the most rigged election in history'. President King recorded 243000 votes in the 1927 election in which only 15000 voters actually took part.

45　The fraternal orders constituted a major mark of class distinction and, for a long time after the 1980 election, they did not operate. To many ordinary people, this was the only way they believed the Americo-Liberians were no longer in power.

But the mainstay of personal rule was control of the patronage system. All executive appointments were at the President's disposal, and there was 'no formal distinction between political and non-political appointments, nor [was] there any formal provision for recruitment and promotion within government departments' (Clapham 1976:37). The President's control extended to ordinary matters like scholarships and deciding who could go abroad to study. An apt summary of the dimensions of patronage control under Tubman, is presented thus:

> He tried, quite successfully, to restrain all independent sources of power. For one thing, he undertook at first to write all official cheques over US$25 (later US$100). His personal 'green letter' appointing or dismissing civil servants became the single most important source of patronage. His personal signature on every transaction involving the sale of land was the passport to wealth and local power for those who wished to acquire land... His surveillance of the educational system and particularly of students going abroad on government and foreign scholarships made clear to the young where their lot was being decided (Lowenkopf 1976:109-110).

Tubman recruited a retinue of 'public relations officers' who, in actual fact, were his personal spies in all the offices. To forestall the creation of any other powerful political base, he reshuffled his cabinet frequently and changed county superintendents often. In the military, police and judiciary and the bureaucracy, loyalty to the President was needed to advance and, to maximise the use of patronage, new positions were constantly created in government departments.

Where patronage and other civil strategies failed to serve the needs of personal rule, there was always a fall-back on coercive instruments which included repressive laws, police brutality, security agencies and the army. Student Movements and labour unions which are universally at the forefront of opposition were closely guided and suppressed. The two labour bodies under Tubman — the Congress of Industrial Organisations and the Labour Congress of Liberia were controlled by government and the TWP. The Congress of Industrial Organisations was once led by Tubman's son, William V. S. Tubman, Jr. Moreover, until 1963, strikes were illegal, and the few strikes before then, like the one in 1961, were suppressed by the army. The threat posed by student and labour unions lay in the fact that they were dominated by African-Liberians. Under Tolbert, with worsening economic conditions, the opposition, built around populist bodies like MOJA and PAL (PPP) became very formidable and this invited even greater repression through arrests and detentions. In 1979, when he was harassed by the rice riots and feared possible overthrow, Tolbert invited

Guinean soldiers to quell the riots (having signed a mutual defence treaty with President Sekou Toure in January 1979).

In all this, as was emphasised earlier on, it was not personal rule *per se* that was important — it was the use to which it was put, first, as the instrument (and arbiter) of Americo-Liberian hegemonic class rule and, second, as the instrument of checking African-Liberian threats.

The Beginnings of the Challenge to Hegemonic Rule

The integration efforts of Tubman and Tolbert paid off handsomely in generating a 'revolutionary consciousness' among the African-Liberians. With increasing number of them receiving education and getting to the threshold of class privileges, but realising that they were the exclusive preserve of the Americo-Liberians, questions began to be raised as to whether the country was for Americo-Liberians only. Many observers expected militant nationalism or at least, an attempt by the African-Liberians to liberate themselves, but they did not. One factor which constantly worked against them in this regard was the gulf which, willy-nilly, the Americo-Liberians had created between the coastal African-Liberians and the hinterland ones. Having been associated with the Americo-Liberians for a long time and having been given crumbs of privileges, there was a feeling of superiority on the part of the coastal groups like the Kru, Grebo and Vai, which, for a long time, prevented them from joining forces with the hinterlanders. The initial challenges to Americo-Liberian hegemony in an integrated Liberia were by the coastal indigenous groups and it took quite a long time before the hinterlanders effectively came into the picture and for a unity to be formed between the two groups. It was when they succeeded in doing this that they were able to overthrow the Americo-Liberian dynasty.

The forms of challenge involved democratic and violent attempts to overthrow the hegemonic class. The democratic attempts involved African-Liberian politicians who were interested in contesting or actually contested the presidential election. There were two notable instances of this and the outcomes were predictably the same: reactions from the ruling class that indicated that presidential power was exclusively for Americo-Liberians. First, in 1931, Momolu Massaquoi, Vai, and an *assimilado* who held diplomatic positions got dismissed from government service and had his name blotted from all public records for daring to express an interest (no more than that) in becoming President (Smyke 1983). Second, in 1951, Didwho Twe, Kru, formed the United Peoples' Party which was mainly

53

Kru-based, to contest the Presidential election against Tubman. The party was refused registration on the grounds of late registration. Twe therefore decided to run on the platform of the Reformation Party, another (coastal) indigenous party formed by Nat-Sie Brownell, Francis Morais and others. In his campaigns, Tubman tried to play down the Americo-Liberian/African-Liberian cleavage which Twe made his major campaign weapon:

> Mr. Twe and his adherents complain that for a hundred and four years of the independence of this country, no aborigine had had the honour of being President of the nation. Who, does he call aborigines, he and his dangling group of a fifth of the Kru tribe? I protest. I contest his supercilious, misconceived notion. H. R. W. Johnson, Daniel Edward Howard... and William V. S. Tubman are all aborigines and indigenous people of this country, for we were all born, bred and reared here (Roberts *et. al.*, 1972:48).

But of course being born and bred in Liberia did not make Tubman an African-Liberian, and he knew it. The real point he was making was that the African-Liberians did not have any claim to power in a country which the Americo-Liberians established for *themselves*. To teach Twe and others like him a lesson, after the election which returned Tubman, he and other leaders of the Reformation Party were charged with sedition and were forced to flee to Sierra-Leone.

The violent attempts to overthrow the hegemonic class, on the other hand, were much more rampant, and took the form of attempted *coup d'état*. Although, it is easy to conclude that the rampancy of these attempts was a reflection of the closure of other channels of political competition, we should be careful because:

> none of the reported coups got very far, and some of them may well have been invented or exaggerated by the government in order to discipline particular politicians whom the President previously wished to cut down to size (Clapham 1976:64).

Nevertheless, they constitute a backdrop against which the coup of 1980 is to be examined because they indicate that quite early in the life of an integrated Liberian, it was clear that, given the stronghold of the Americo-Liberians on state power, and their unwillingness to relinquish it through democratic means, violent overthrow provided the only available option. The first notable instance of this form of challenge was in 1940 when President Edwin Barclay accused several African-Liberian leaders including Nathaniel Massaquoi of planning to violently overthrow the ruling class and assassinate the President. In his evidence during the trial, Massaquoi admitted that a youth association was formed in 1937 whose sole aim 'was to place aborigines in the government of the country permanently', but denied any plan to assassinate Barclay. He and others charged along with him, notably Kollie S. Tamba and Frank Tarr Grimes were found guilty of treason and convicted. It is interesting to know that, in pursuance of expanding his support-constituency to include the African-Liberians, Tubman released these men from prison and proceeded to appoint them to top government positions: Massaquoi became a Judge and later Education Minister and Tamba was made Counsellor in the Ministry of Foreign Affairs.

The 1960s and early 1970s were particularly replete with the 'uncovering' of coup plots. In 1962, Tubman accused anti-government students of plotting to overthrow him. In 1963, Colonel D. Y. Thompson, Grebo and acting Commander of the National Guard, was accused, along with several other Grebo, Vai and Kru soldiers of planning a coup at the instigation of external forces (Tubman actually had Nkrumah in mind in making this allegation.).[46] In 1966, at the height of a countrywide workers' strike, another plot was 'uncovered' which involved former Vice President C. L. Simpson (who was half African-Liberian), former Attorney-General Joseph Chesson, and several African-Liberian leaders. In 1968, Ambassador Henry B. Fahnbulleh, Vai, was accused of attempting to mount an ethnic movement against the government. The significance of this plot was the fact that it was the first time hinterland African-Liberians were mentioned in a coup and, moreover, in league with coastlanders. Fahnbulleh was tried along with the Superintendents of Lofa, Bong and Nimba counties for treason. He was found guilty and imprisoned, while his personal property was confiscated. He was later pardoned by Tolbert and appointed assistant Minister of State for Presidential affairs.

Then in 1970, General G.T. Washington, Kru and former Chief of Staff was alleged to have planned to assassinate the Secretary of Defence. Finally, in 1973, Tolbert 'uncovered' another plot involving the Minister of defence, Prince Brown, two indigenous Lieutenant-Colonels and several African-Liberians, mainly from hinterland groups who were later found guilty of plotting to kill the President and his brother. Following this coup, about 700 officers and men of the 4,000 strong army, almost all African-Liberian, were retired. The problem with these various attempts, as

---

46   At this time, Nkrumah was considered a threat by conservative African leaders because they feared that his advocacy of a United States of Africa had, as part of its modus operandi, the installation of loyal governments in place of those like Tubman who opposed his grand plans.

we have said, is that, coming only from government and the President himself, it is difficult to substantiate them. But they did indicate that the army was potentially the institution through which the African-Liberians could overthrow the hegemonic class. This potentiality was not lost during both the Tubman and Tolbert as they closely controlled appointments and promotions in the army and appointed only trusted and loyal officers to sensitive positions. In January 1979, Tolbert signed a mutual defence pact with Guinea partly because he feared he could lose control over the military which was becoming increasingly a hotbed of indigenous plots and 'revolutionary consciousness'. What seemed to be lacking was an enabling environment and, by the time it was created in 1980, there were at least two coups in the offing, both led by African-Liberians.[47]

The Eclipse of Hegemonic Rule

Throughout the 1960s and 1970s, it was clear that hegemonic rule, hinged on Americo-Liberian control, could not continue to be sustained for much longer. The phenomenal increase in the number of opposition movements under various guises as well as sustained acts of civil disobedience and disorder gave the grounds for this optimism. What heightened the tempo of opposition activities was the decay of the state marked by its economic retrenchment and repression. Under the circumstances, was it possible for the opposition groups to remain exclusively African-Liberians because, afterall, the economic retrenchment affected all Liberians and not only African-Liberians? For many authors, part of the answer lies in the fact that the Liberian state was no longer exclusively Americo-Liberian, as the African-Liberian component of government and privileged classes had become substantial (Liebenow 1987; Clapham 1989). This did not however, mean the end of hegemonic rule by the Americo-Liberians who admitted African-Liberians into the privileged ranks only on the basis of the latter agreeing to be a local-comprador class. From the point of hegemony therefore, the ruling class did not really change from being Americo-Liberian based. In fact, the quick acceptance of Doe's government by African-Liberian TWP bigwigs could be explained in terms of their own

---

47   One was the coup by Doe which was carried through. The other was by Colonel William Jerbo, Loma, who was believed to be planning his own coup by the time Doe struck. He subsequently attempted to flee to Sierra-Leone because Doe's PRC saw him as a threat. He died in the process.

eagerness to be liberated from hegemonic rule, though the fact that there was no social reproduction outside the state gave little option to them.

What of the opposition groups themselves, did they remain exclusively African-Liberian? Of course, they did not, just as all opposition to hegemonic rule had not only been by African-Liberians (there were several cases of intraclass conflicts, but these have been eclipsed by the focus on African-Liberian/Americo-Liberian conflicts).[48] In other words, opposition to hegemonic rule all through Liberian history was not exclusively by African-Liberians, and in the 1970s, it was not. But the size of Americo-Liberian opposition which joined the more populous African-Liberian ones was very small and could be considered negligible. What was interesting about Americo-Liberian opposition elements was the fact that they were foreign-based and concentrated mainly in the United States of America.[49] In these places, they easily joined forces with African-Liberians who were either studying or living abroad. Within Liberia itself, except for a few radical ones at the University of Liberia, Americo-Liberian membership of opposition movements was negligible. Another interesting fact about the few Americo-Liberian members of the opposition groups was that almost all of them had African-Liberian mothers and were of original Congo stock. This fact helped to eliminate mutual suspicions and distrust between them and the African-Liberians. It goes without saying that these ones were at the lowest rungs of Americo-Liberian hegemony and therefore had sufficient motivation to want to overthrow it. But, as we have said, their number was quite negligible, and this made the opposition groups predominantly African-Liberian based. Predictably, they were led by the indigenous educated elite who suffered most from the discriminatory practices of hegemonic rule.

In the 1970s, several opposition groups emerged. Most of them based at the University of Liberia. The most notable and active of these were MOJA, PAL and later, after it transformed into a political party, PPP, students unions and other radical bodies. MOJA, which began as an Africa-wide organisation, was formed in 1973 by University lecturers — Amos Sawyer and Togba-Nah Tipoteh of the University of Liberia and Dew Mayson of

---

48   Further research is needed to address issues like this, as we shall argue in the concluding chapter.

49   This was because many Americo-Liberian families continued to maintain ties with their Kith in the United States of America.

57

Cuttington University College.[50] It aimed at promoting democratic principles and practices and checking arbitrary rule in Liberia and elsewhere in Africa (Taryor 1985). MOJA hoped to become registered as a political party, and Sawyer strengthened opposition consciousness when he declared his intention to contest election for the Mayoralty of Monrovia in 1980. An affiliate of MOJA, the Susukuu social movement, was very active in the popular struggle, having in its membership students, port and factory workers, peasants and the intelligentsia. Kamara (1986:105) has articulated the role of the Susukuu thus: 'As a national social movement, Susukuu popularised the political struggles urged against the Liberian state by the progressive elements... of different community-based organisations opposed to the ruling class'. One of the most militant community-based organisations which was established with Susukuu support was the Putu Development Corporation (PUDECO) in the Putu chiefdom of Grand Gedeh county. By encouraging and mobilising several community-based associations, the Susukuu movement helped to integrate the urban and rural elements of the popular struggle against hegemonic rule.

The other major opposition movement was PAL which was formed in 1973 as an association of Liberian students studying in the United States of America. It shifted base to Liberia in the late 1970s when many of its leaders like Baccus Matthews, Oscar Quiah and Chea Cheapoo returned home, and adopted a strategy of confrontation with government. This strategy and the group's perception as a socialist movement made its initial attempt at becoming a political party under the name PPP fail. PAL, whose membership was predominantly students provided the vanguard of the protests which degenerated to full-scale rioting following the increase in the price of a bag of rice, the country's staple food, from US$22 to US$30 in April 1979. This riot which was put down by military force, was the turning point in the victory of the popular forces over the hegemonic class. As tension increased and Tolbert's coercive instruments were mobilised at full blast, Baccus Matthews called his members to embark on a general strike and demanded the immediate resignation of Tolbert's government in March 1980. Matthews and other PPP leaders were promptly arrested and were to be tried for treason. The nation-wide tension generated by this development provided the opportunity for the coup of 12 April 1980 to take place.

---

50   It has been suggested that MOJA functionaries feared state repression, and that was why
      they chose to make it an Africa-wide organisation.

4 - The 1980 Coup and its Aftermath

In this Chapter, we examine the coup of 12 April 1980 which not only violently ended over one hundred years of Americo-Liberian hegemonic rule, but also, in its aftermath, transformed the arena of ethnic politics in dramatic ways. This event has been described as Liberia's own version of independence from colonial rule because it liberated African-Liberians and gave them control of state power.[51] Henceforth, attention was to be focused on the African-Liberians themselves, and how successfully they were able to manage the newly acquired power. Americo-Liberians and leading commentators had argued all along that a government controlled by them was unlikely to be stable because of the deep-seated conflicts amongst them which the Americo-Liberians tried unsuccessfully to curb.[52] Were the events which followed the coup and eventually led to the civil war which broke out in 1989 therefore an act of self-fulfilling prophecy? Why was it impossible for the African-Liberians to sustain the unity which a century-long Americo-Liberian domination had forced on them? Would the situation have been different if the Americo-Liberians were overthrown by democratic means, or if another soldier rather than Doe emerged as Head of State? What was the role of the Americo-Liberians in all this: did they accept their overthrow or did they seek to re-establish the old order? These and several other questions are the focus of this chapter.

Interpreting the 1980 Coup

In Chapter 3, we concluded that because of the unwillingness of the Americo-Liberians to relinquish power or to open access to presidential power to the African-Liberians through democratic means, violent overthrow which had a long history of unsuccessful attempts provided the only alternative to the African-Liberians to liberate themselves. The major reason why previous attempts were unsuccessful was the absence of an enabling environment. On the one hand, there continued to be schisms between the coastal and hinterland natives and, on the other, popular

---

51   As in most other postcolonial states in Africa, however, the basic colonial structures of government remained unchanged.

52   As we argued and demonstrated in Chapter 2, these conflicts were galvanised by the coming of Americo-Liberian settlers.

consciousness for the overthrow was neither sufficiently aroused nor mobilised. Events of the late 1970s which saw formidable and populist opposition by MOJA, PAL (PPP) and others changed all that. These groups were helped by the economic retrenchment of the state which afforded them the opportunity to mobilise the masses against Tolbert's government. By the time the rice riots took place in 1979, many expected the downfall of government. But it survived, and became more desperate in its efforts to keep the old order. This gingered greater opposition and, by March 1980, the opposition leaders felt formidable enough to ask Tolbert to resign! When Baccus Matthews and others were arrested and awaiting trial for treason (for attempting to organise a nation-wide general strike), the army seized the opportunity of discontent and mass resolve to bring down the Tolbert government 'in the cause of the people'. The coup was organised by seventeen soldiers of the non-commissioned ranks led by Master Sergeant Samuel Doe (see Table 3). They were all African-Liberians, with the majority being 'up-country' (hinterland) boys. It was a very bloody overthrow which saw the assassination of President Tolbert and the execution of twelve other top-ranking Americo-Liberians.

Table 3: Ethnic Identities of the 1980 Coupists

Name	Rank	Ethnic Group
Samuel K. Doe	Master Sergeant	Krahn
Thomas Weh Syen	Sergeant	Sapo
Nicholas Podier	Corporal	Grebo
Henry S. Zuo	Sergeant	Gio
Thomas Quiwonkpa	Sergeant	Gio
David Karmai	Sergeant	Gio
Swen N. Dixon	Sergeant	Kru
Jerry Gban	Sergeant	Krahn
Jacob Swen	Corporal	Kru
Fallah Varney	Corporal	Kissi
Jerry Jorwley	Corporal	Grebo
Harris S. Johnson	Corporal	Krahn
Larry W. Borteh	Corporal	Kru
Robert B. Nowoku	Corporal	Loma
Harrison Pennue	Corporal	Krahn
Robert Zuo	Private First Class	Gio
William Gould	Private First Class	Krahn

Source: Dunn and Holsoe (1985)

Several attempts have been made to interpret the 1980 coup. The most popular explanation given is that the soldiers acted on behalf of the African-Liberians to overthrow the 'colonial' masters. The facts that all the organisers of the coup were African-Liberians who adopted the slogan 'in the cause of people'; that the People's Redemption Council (PRC) which became the instrument of the new government comprised only African-Liberians; and that the African-Liberian members of the Tolbert regime and the TWP were quickly incorporated into the new government while their Americo-Liberian counterparts were harassed or forced to flee the country are often cited in support of this interpretation. Furthermore, although Doe took care not to be sectional in his speeches, there were indications that the coup was planned to 'liberate' the African-Liberians from time to time. At take-over, he said:

> We are beginning this new government with much knowledge and experience about the great injustices suffered by the masses of our people. We are entering this new part of Liberian history with a strong sense of those acts of previous governments which have held our people down for too long... We seek to build a new society in which there is justice, human dignity, equal opportunities and fair treatment for all... '

On another occasion of a special message to the nation in 1980, he said:

> For too long did the masses of our people live in their own country, only to be treated like slaves in a plantation. For too long have our suffering people cried out for freedom, only to be put behind the bars of oppression; for nearly one hundred years, our people...were not considered as citizens under the laws of our country.

Then, of course, there was the fact that, whether Doe said so or not, the African-Liberians saw the coup as their own take-over of power. They urged Doe to complete the take-over process by changing the national symbols, including the name of the country. Though Doe failed to do this, there was no doubt about their sense of liberation, something they looked forward to for several decades.[53]

Do these facts make the coup a 'nationalist' revolution? The answer, surprisingly, has to be a cautious yes, because, as later events showed, Doe and his collaborators were simply opportunists who exploited the situation

---

53   As Sawyer described the situation in an interview with *West Africa* (17 November, 1980): 'The major change is the breaking of a century old alienation for the masses of the people. If you were in Monrovia ... you would see in spite of economic crunch that there (was) an air of liberation... a new dignity. In essence, this is the major development that cannot be reversed'.

to pursue personal and selfish interests. In other words, the coup was not really 'in the cause of the people'; it was 'in the cause of Doe (and his collaborators)'. The irreversible political development it brought, however, was the other-throw of Americo-Liberian hegemonic rule — at least that meant African-Liberian ascendancy to power; it was another matter what Doe decided to do with this power.

~Which brings us to the second popular interpretation of the coup, that it hijacked the revolution from the popular organisations. Nyong'o (1987) describes it as a 'stolen revolution' or a 'counter-revolution' while Tipoteh (1982) regards it as an 'abortion' of the plans MOJA and the others had for the 1983 elections. Elsewhere, he has further asserted that 'the principal objective of the military take over... was to destabilise the work of MOJA and abort the struggle of the Liberian people for democracy...' (Tipoteh 1985). By organising the rice riots of 1979 and calling for a general strike in 1980, at least, the popular organisations not only demonstrated their wide support, but also their readiness to confront the government, and fight it to resignation. The transformation of PAL into PPP and the decision by Sawyer, to contest the Mayoralty of Monrovia should therefore be seen as part of the process of overthrowing the established order.[54] Except it can be proven that these groups played a part in the planning and execution of the coup, and they did not: the inevitable conclusion to be reached is that the soldiers capitalised on the process of overthrow already initiated by PPP and MOJA to seize power, much in the same way that the soldiers in Mali exploited the popular protests situation in 1990 to seize power.

· However, Doe quickly recognised that in addition to sloganeering that the take over of government was 'in the cause of the people', one way to legitimise his government, and increase its popularity was to align with the radical elements. Moreover, being barely literate, as were the other 'revolutionaries', Doe came to rely on them for the intellectual needs of governance.[55] Largely for these reasons, he released PPP leaders from detention and appointed key leaders of popular groups into government: Baccus Matthews, Oscar Quiah and Chea Cheagoo (PPP) and Togba-Nah

---

54   However, Clapham (1989:107) doubts if these groups had the organisational capacity needed to overthrow the regime. He certainly overlooks the activities of these groups in 1979 and 1980.

55   It is said, for instance, that Professor Sawyer led other intellectuals to advice Doe and write his speeches at the early part of his regime. Charles Taylor is also said to have served in a consultative capacity, having been a radical student in the United States of America (*West Africa*, 12 August 1990).

Tipoteh and Boima Fahnbulleh (MOJA) were made Ministers of major departments: foreign affairs, planning and economic development, justice, etc. In addition, there were many other radical elements who served in less conspicuous but no less important capacities.[56] Then there were the student organisations with which Doe openly fraternised at the initial part of his administration.

But the alliances did not last long. A few months into the new era, Doe parted ways with the radical and popular forces. He began with students whom he accused of lacking discipline. When the Liberian National Students Union (LINSU) produced a charter of demands asking Doe to redress Krahn domination in the composition of the PRC and, calling, amongst others, for a redistribution of land and hand-over of power to civilians, the views were considered too radical and their leaders, including Commony Wisseh, were clamped into detention.[57] Next, he turned on MOJA and PPP. He began by removing their members from his administration and replacing them with powerful members of the overthrown TWP regime, and then appointing the TWP men to key positions: Jackson Doe, formally TWP Vice-Chairman and Senator was made Adviser on national and international affairs; George Boley, formerly member of TWP task force (think tank); was made minister; Bernard Blamo minister of education under Tolbert was appointed Managing Director of National Ports Authority and later minister of State for Presidency; Edward Massaquoi, Director of Special Security Service under Tolbert was appointed Chairman, Joint Security Forces; others like Emmanuel Shaw, Charles Sherman, Ernest Eastmann, Scott Toweh, Troho Kparghai, Edward Kesselly, Emmanuel Gardiner, Patrick Minikon and John Rancy were appointed into key offices. The return of the TWP regime became so established that one commentator described Doe's government as 'TWP government stage two' (Anon 1983). Along the same lines, Clapham (1989) has described Doe's government as 'a bastard descendant of its predecessor', while Nyong'o (1987:209-210) believes Doe merely restored the 'old order', but with him and his cohorts on the 'political driving seat'. Assessments like these however, fail to see that the TWP big wigs that Doe aligned with were almost completely African-Liberians. As such, it was not really the old order that was restored; it was simply a case of promoting the

56 One of these was Charles Taylor.
57 Repression of students' groups increased as more and more progressive bodies were banned.

African-Liberian section of the TWP from the back seat to the front seat, which accorded well with the revolutionary change.

But why did Doe embark on the *volte-face*, or was he simply showing the true colour of his 'revolution' which was hidden at coup-time? To answer these questions, we need to appreciate the fact that Doe's search was for a base on which he could consolidate his power. At the beginning, this base was obviously to be found in the popular groups. But Doe would not allow them take over control of his government. Thus, when Tipoteh resigned from government on the grounds that Doe was destroying the revolution by appointing TWP politicians into it, Doe let it be known that his government was being run by the PRC and not PPP or MOJA! Much later, at his 33rd birthday celebration in 1985, Doe denied any association with these groups, and argued that they did not play any part in the coup that brought him to power.[58] Rather than continue to be dependent on radicals who were not prepared to play second-fiddle, Doe quickly changed his power-base to the opportunistic African-Liberian section of the TWP which was desperate to cling to state power and therefore willing to play second-fiddle. Of course, second-fiddle or not, once he consolidated his power, Doe became intolerant of any shade of opposition, and this was extended to the TWP chiefs.

This leaves us with the interpretation of the coup as something undertaken by a group of soldiers who were hungry for power,[59] but who, at the same time and independent of their motives, played the historical role of overthrowing Americo-Liberian hegemonic rule. The latter helped to make the problem of their acceptability easier but once that stage was passed, the true colour of Doe's 'revolution' was exposed: tyrannical rule at the worst. This character of the military government of Doe and its palpable lack of positive direction and good management after intellectuals and technocrats were expelled from the government, made supposedly Africa-Liberian ascendancy something of an anti-climax. A democratic government would

---

58 In a post-mortem, Sawyer says of the *grand deceit* of Doe: 'We were all rather deceived by the military coup of 1980, seeing in it, at first, an element for progressive movement, but later realising that it was nothing but a recipe for a tyrannical rule' (*African Concord*, 10 December 1990).

59 In an interview in 1985, Doe gives the impression that he was an unwilling President and that the 1980 coup was planned simply to put an end to Americo-Liberian oppression, no more. (Africa Now, May 1985). But his performance as Head of State and his subsequent decision to transform himself into a civilian President show clearly that the hunger for power was a major propeller of the coup.

have made a lot of difference, but Doe's delay in returning to civil rule which saw him continuing in power again thwarted this possibility.

The Aftermath of the Coup

The aftermath of the coup which, as we have said, ended Americo-Liberian hegemonic rule, witnessed dramatic changes in the terrain and character of ethnic conflicts. As was the case in other newly independent African states where the conflicts changed from that between the colonised and the colonisers to that amongst the formally colonised peoples themselves, the situation in Liberia changed radically from African-Liberian/Americo-Liberian conflict to African-Liberian/African-Liberian conflict. However, this development did not immediately follow the coup because during the initial part of Doe's administration, when there were populist pretensions, elements of a 'united' front not simply against the former Americo-Liberian overlords but more importantly to preserve the new order (against possible Americo-Liberian attempts to stage a come-back or to prove to the world that the African-Liberians were capable of governing themselves) could be discerned.[60] Doe's turn-around to embrace elements of the old regime as well as his calculated measures to keep himself in power by all means turned attention away from the Americo-Liberian enemy, (who, for the majority of African-Liberians nevertheless remained an enemy) to the 'enemies' within the African-Liberians themselves. This involved intra-African-Liberian conflicts and struggles for power and privileges which took the forms of struggles amongst members of the military government (whom ethnic followers perceived as representing ethnic interests), coup d'etats (which also had ethnic characters) and inter-party competition. As before, the object of these conflicts was control of the government which was the major access to wealth, privileges and other forms of patronage. As previously disadvantaged and excluded groups, the desperation to make up for previous losses heightened the new forms of ethnic conflicts. The perception by most of them that Doe wanted all the power and privileges for only himself and his Krahn group worsened the situation.

---

60   This was why, for a long time, key Americo-Liberians who escaped death in 1980 were kept under surveillance.

Unlike most other countries in Africa, where the colonisers left the scene to the colonised, however, the Americo-Liberians were only overthrown, not driven out of the country. While it is true that they were excluded from many organs of government and, in particular, the PRC, and that conflicts among African-Liberians eclipsed their own activities, it is both misleading and dangerous to assume that they were no longer joined in the struggle for state power. As we emphasised at the beginning of this study, the temptation to think that the conflicts in post-coup Liberia which led to the civil war were simply Krahn-Mano/Gio, for example, even when on the surface, they presented such characters, must be resisted. This is because the Americo-Liberian elements never left the conflict action-set. Those who fled abroad, especially to the United States of America formed pressure groups which struggled to influence American policy towards Liberia and to arouse international public opinion against the Doe regime. Several times, they succeeded in convincing the United States of America officials to make democratisation and release of political detainees conditions for aid on which Doe's regime greatly depended. Some of these groups also nursed the ambition of coming home to take over power from Doe, and it is instructive to note that the movement by Charles Taylor which eventually led to the civil war had a solid Americo-Liberian support-base at the beginning. The major strategy in this endeavour was to exploit existing conflicts, especially, that between the Krahn and the Gio/Mano to further their interests. We shall have more to say on this in Chapter 5.

The Aftermath: An Outline

Before we begin to examine, in closer details, how and why ethnic conflicts in the Doe years worsened, we need to be familiar with the events that took place in the aftermath of the coup and the social and economic factors which underlay them. One way of summarising these events is to say that they centred around the strategies and tactics employed by Doe to keep himself in power. He systematically eliminated all the other sixteen 'revolutionaries' with whom he seized power, repressed all forms of opposition and transformed himself from a military dictator to a civilian dictator in 1985. After surviving numerous attempts to oust him, including two coups by Thomas Quiwonkpa,[61] Doe was finally killed in the thick of

---

61   Doe claimed to have survived thirty-two coup attempts.

the civil war which we shall examine in Chapter 5. The main events of the Doe years can be discussed under the following headings.

Doe First, Doe Last

As indicated above, Doe systematically eliminated all rival claimants to power and suppressed, in a more ferocious manner than previous Liberian leaders, all shades of opposition. To begin with, he eliminated the sixteen other 'revolutionaries' with whom he staged the 1980 coup and who became members of the PRC. In August 1981, five PRC members including Thomas Weh Syen, its former Deputy-Chairman were executed on the grounds that they were plotting to overthrow Doe. Doe and Syen reportedly fell out over the issue of whether or not to maintain neutrality in external relations.[62] In 1983, Doe fell out with Thomas Quiwonkpa whom many considered the strongman of the regime, and demoted him from Commanding General of the army to Secretary-General of the PRC.[63] Quiwonkpa organised an unsuccessful coup later that year, after which he fled to the United States of America. He returned in 1985 to organise another coup on the platform of the National Patriotic Front of Liberia. This time, he was nearly successful, but lost his life to the bargain. Nicholas Podier who replaced Syen as Deputy-Chairman of PRC was arrested in 1984, and in 1985, the Deputy Commander of the Executive Mansion Guard was executed after being found 'guilty' of plotting to assassinate Doe. The major effect these eliminations had was that the ethnic groups to which these PRC members belonged, which saw them as their own access to state power, withdrew their support for Doe (see Table 4 for the ethnic identities of the PRC members). The confrontation with fellow revolutionaries which proved to be most enduring and disastrous in ethnic terms was that which Doe had with Quiwonkpa. The coups organised by the latter, and the degeneration in the conflicts between the Mano/Gio and Krahn they resulted in, were the fore-runners to the civil war.

---

62   Syen favoured the retention of non-alignment in foreign policy, but this was not the reason for his execution.

63   Quiwonkpa reportedly rejected the new position because he saw himself as a professional soldier.

Table 4: Ethnic Identities of PRC Members

Name	Status in PRC	Ethnic Group
Samuel K Doe	Chairman	Krahn
Thomas W Syen	Co-Chairman	Sapo
Nicholas Podier	Speaker	Grebo
Thomas Quiwonkpa	Senior Member	Gio
Fallah Varney	Senior Member	Kissi
Jerry C Jorwley	Senior Member	Grebo
Larry W Borteh	Senior Member	Kru
Abraham D Kollie	Senior Member	Loma
Robert Sumo	Member	Loma
Albert Toe	Member	Krahn
Harris S Johnson	Member	Krahn
Henry Zuo	Member	Gio
Jacob Swen	Member	Kru
Nelson Toe	Member	Krahn
William Gould	Member	Krahn
Kolonseh Gonyor	Member	Gio
Jeffry Gbatu	Member	Mano
David Karmai	Co-Member	Gio
Harrison Pennue	Co-Member	Krahn
Jerry Gban	Co-Member	Krahn
Joseph Sampson	Co-Member	Grebo
Robert B Nowoku	Co-Member	Loma
Robert Zuo	Co-Member	Gio
Joseph Tubman	Co-Member	Grebo
Swen Divon	Co-Member	Kru
John Nyumah	Co-Member	?
Yellah Kebah	Co-Member	?
Stanley Tanwuo	Co-Member	?

Source: Schroder and Korte (1986:44).

Doe's suppression and elimination tactics were extended to other radical and progressive persons and groups in the country. One of his first decrees banned all political activities and groups, including MOJA and PPP and another abolished strikes. The University of Liberia (and other educational institutions) were not spared because they were regarded as the hotbeds of radical opposition. In August 1984 and several times afterwards, the University was closed down for anti-government activities after soldiers had sacked the campus and had the President, Vice-Presidents, Council and

Senate members dismissed. That same year, 300 elementary and high school teachers were sacked for being socialist. In November 1985, following Quiwonkpa's failed coup, radical organisations including the Press Union of Liberia, Students' Council of University of Liberia and National Union of Liberian teachers were banned while opposition politicians, including Ellen Johnson-Sirleaf, Jackson Doe, Gabriel Kpolleh and Edward Kesselly were arrested and detained. The press was also intimidated. There was the notorious Decree 88A which forbade the spreading of lies, untruths, and unproved claims under which newspapers like the *Daily Observer*, *Footprints Today* and *Sun Times* were proscribed or suspended, and journalists were arrested, jailed or simply killed, like Charles Gbenyon.

Doe's transformation to a civilian President did little to change his dictatorship because he remained essentially a military ruler (his civilian ministers were given forced commissioned ranks in the armed forces of Liberia).[64] Under the civilian dispensation, his repressive focus was on the opposition parties — registered and non-registered — which challenged his election in 1985 and, thereafter, sought to pursue a policy of civil uncooperation.

Doe's rapacious tactics to remain in power by all means make nonsense of any analysis which suggests that his government was a TWP stage-two government. Like the people and the popular fronts, the African-Liberian TWP machinery was simply another constituency ladder he could climb to consolidate his power. Once he did that, it was clear to everyone that Doe, not the TWP, was in charge, notwithstanding that his National Democratic Party of Liberia (NDPL) had important TWP members. By 1986, Doe had fallen out of favour with everyone else except his Krahn people whom he appointed to most sensitive security and military positions. This personal/Krahn domination of state power further impelled the other groups to opposition.

Transition to the Second Republic

Under pressure from the United States of America which made the granting of aid contingent upon a definite commitment to return to civilian rule, Doe promised a return to civil rule quite early in the life of his regime. From within the country, popular fronts now represented by students

---

64   Doe preferred to be called Commander-in-Chief to being called (only) President.

organisations[65] were urging a quick return to civil rule, as were radicals like Sawyer, Tipoteh, Matthews, who saw in such a scheme, an opportunity to carry out the revolutionary plans they had when Doe hijacked the change process.

Doe launched the transition to civil rule in 1981 when he instituted a twenty-five member National Constitution Drafting Committee (CONCOM) under the Chairmanship of Professor Amos Sawyer, Dean of Liberia College and notable MOJA leader. To allay fears of possible biases in the composition of CONCOM, Doe declared at its inauguration that the members had 'been carefully selected to reflect our national political and social realities... Regional balance, professional balance, technical competence... have been significant criteria considered in their selection'.[66] The terms of reference of the Committee included to review the 1847 Constitution, study the political and social problems related to it, and incorporate useful ideas from relevant comparative experiences. The review involved public discussions and debates, submission of memoranda or what was called 'hearings' by interested persons and bodies, as well as visits to West African countries which, around the time, had just completed re-civilianisation programmes: Nigeria, Ghana and Sierra Leone. In CONCOM's view, there was nothing fundamentally wrong with the 1847 Constitution except in those areas which still appeared to suggest that African-Liberians were second-class citizens; what was wrong was the inability of the Constitution to prevent the emergence of one party regimes or military take over of government.

Along these lines, the draft constitution outlawed military coups and provided, in the section on political parties that 'laws, regulations, decrees or measures which might have the effect of creating a one-party state shall be declared unconstitutional'. Another major issue CONCOM dealt with was that of national integration. The preamble to the Constitution was amended to read, *inter alia* that: 'all of our people, irrespective of their history, traditions and ethnic background, are part of one common body politic'. A new chapter was also introduced on 'General Principles of National Policy'[67] which clearly followed the lines of 'The Directive

---

65 At this time, most other groups had either been co-opted or driven underground.

66 CONCOM had nine academics, including professors of Law and the social sciences, two business executives and three senior civil servants, amongst others.

67 This chapter spelt out the philosophy and directions of integrative policies to be pursued by government.

Principles of State Policy' which was an innovation in the 1979 Constitution of the Federal Republic of Nigeria. The chapter provided guidelines on important matters like fostering national integration, preserving and promoting cultural values and checking ethnicity and sectionalism. Tubman (1986:113) however, believes that a lot more than constitutional entries was needed to achieve these lofty goals.[68] In most other areas, particularly in the area of the system of government, the draft Constitution retained the provision of the 1847 constitution with only slight amendments.[69]

Sawyer's Commission submitted the draft constitution in March 1983. Next, a fifty-nine member Constitution Advisory Assembly composed of representatives of political subdivisions and chaired by Edward Kesselly was inaugurated at Gbarnga to review the draft 'article by article and propose amendments, and honestly advise the PRC on whether the document should be accepted or rejected' (Givens 1986). The Assembly submitted its report in which it virtually ratified the draft constitution in October 1983. Meanwhile, the Special Electoral Commission (SECOM) had been created to compile the voters register, formulate criteria and guidelines for registering political parties, delineate constituencies, formulate electoral laws and conduct elections. The Commission was headed by Emmet Harmon, an influential Americo-Liberian politician who had served under Tubman and Tolbert. On July 3, 1983, SECOM conducted a referendum at which the new constitution was ratified by the vast majority of Liberians. The constitution then came into effect.

The next stage in the transition process was the dissolution of the PRC in June 1984, and its replacement by a transitional ruling body appropriately called Interim National Assembly (INA). The new Assembly comprised members of the dissolved PRC and thirty-one civilian representatives from the counties and other political subdivisions. Much to everyone's surprise, Doe emerged as President of the INA and this made many good readers of the situation begin to suspect that he was unwilling to relinquish power.

The ban on political activities which had been in force since April 1980 was lifted at the end of July 1984. Several political parties emerged, but they first had to meet SECOM's criteria for registering parties, which included having at least 3000 members in no less than six countries, and

---

68   The other requirements involved transforming the social terrain of politics, which could not be done constitutionally.

69   It retained the America-style executive presidential system.

being able to pay a fee of US$50,000 and sureties in property and bond worth US$100,000, and being acceptable to Doe himself. Of the several parties, only four — the National Democratic Party of Liberian (NDPL) whose Chairman (Keikura Kpoto) and Secretary (George Saigbe Boley) were ex-TWP, as were most other members, including Emmet Harmon and Ernest Eastmann, and which had Doe himself as standard bearer; Unity Party (UP) led by Edward Kesselly who was also the standard bearer; Liberia Action Party (LAP) led by Tuan Wreh, with Jackson Fiah Doe as standard bearer; and Liberian Unity Party (LUP) led by William G. Kpolleh who was also the standard bearer — were registered. Other parties, like the Convention Democratic Party led by Wade Appleton, National Integration Party led by Sumo Jones and First All-Integrated Republican Party led by Edwin Dunbar were not registered while Amos Sawyers' Liberian Peoples' Party (LPP) and Baccus Matthews' United Peoples Party which had the most formidable support bases following their MOJA and PPP roots were banned on the grounds of radical politics.[70]

The significance of the line-up of parties was two-fold; one, all the presidential candidates were African-Liberians which was a reflection of the relegation of the Americo-Liberians in the new dispensation, and, two, it was the first time most hinterland African-Liberians were participation in the election of the country's leaders.[71] What could count as the third aspect of the significance of the configuration of parties, is that it was the first time in the history of the country that, as many parties were contesting elections does not come out well because the conduct of the elections and the manner in which government was run thereafter suggest that the multiparty outlook was merely cosmetic.[72]

In the electoral campaigns, ethnicity did not feature as a salient issue, as none of the politicians wanted to be seen to be sectional. The focus was on national issues, the most prominent of which were national unity, human rights, and the economy. Although there were complaints and evidences of intimidation and harassment of the other parties by Doe and the NDPL, the campaigns went on fairly well. Then, finally came the elections in October 1985. The elections were for the Presidency and legislative seats. The latter

---

70   This was an integral part of Doe's plan to ensure an 'easy' victory.
71   As it turned out, however, it was not their participation that ultimately determined who would rule.
72   As we have said, Liberian political system under civilian rule is characterised by the one-party de facto system.

involved elections into twenty-six seats in the Senate (the thirteen counties had two senators each) and sixty-four in the House of Representatives.[73] The official result of the Presidential election showed that Doe secured about 51 per cent of the total votes cast, winning in all but two of the counties (MarGibi and Nimba). The other parties contested this result, alleging irregularities and manipulations by SECOM in favour of Doe, and the popular view was that Jackson Doe of LAP who came second, (see Table 5), actually won the election. The NDPL won overwhelming majorities (53 of 64 seats in the House of Representatives and 22 of 26 seats in the Senate). To all intents and purposes, the country was back to the one-party *de facto* days of TWP hegemony.

Table 5: Results of the 1985 Presidential Election

Standard Bearer	Party	Valid Votes Cast
Samuel K. Doe	NDPL	518,872
Jackson F. Doe	LAP	264,364
William G. Kpolleh	LUP	59,965
Edward B. Kesselly	UP	57,273

Source: Givens (1986:113).

The 'defeated' parties rejected the results and called for fresh elections. They also directed their members not to take up the legislative seats they won.[74] Unfortunately, before matters could be properly sorted out, Quiwonkpa struck in November and came very near to overthrowing Doe. The party leaders were promptly arrested and detained in the notorious Post Stockade and Bella Yella prisons, on suspicion of collusion with Quiwonkpa. Upon their release in 1986, they continued the politics of civil uncooperation which became the hallmark of Liberian politics until the civil war broke out. At some points, they tried to forge a united opposition front. In 1986, for example, they formed the Grand Coalition which had Gabriel Kpolleh as President to forestall the collapse of the opposition. The coalition even included Baccus Matthews' banned UPP. Doe responded by banning the coalition and arresting its leaders. It took the United States of America's

---

73   Only the NDPL fielded candidates for all the legislative seats.
74   Bye-elections were later arranged by SECOM which the parties also boycotted, thus leaving the scene free to the NDPL to control the Senate and House of Representatives.

threat, to stop aid to Liberia if the opposition was not tolerated, for Doe to release the leaders and agree to negotiate with the other parties.[75]

Apart from constantly arresting and detaining members of these opposition parties, another strategy Doe used quite well was that of 'co-optation'. Here, his main weapon was the reliance of the elites on the state for social reproduction, and it worked for him at those times when he penetrated the ranks of the opposition parties, and broke the strength of opposition.[76] What kept opposition going however, was the tying in of the continued existence of opposition to the granting of aid by the United States of America (this was in part because of the Liberian associations based there).

The Political Economy

The point was established in Chapter 2 that the Liberian economy is basically fragile and badly exposed to foreign control. The country had continuously remained a debtor country since 1870 when it took the first loan from European creditors. In addition to dependence of foreign aid and loans, the Liberian economy has also been continuously controlled by foreigners: rubber and iron ore, the major export commodities of the country have remained in foreign hands (Firestone, LAMCO and others) while retail trade which is the mainstay of the domestic economy has been controlled by Lebanese, Syrians and Indians. The other point we noted about Liberian economy in Chapter 2 was that no matter the boom it enjoyed — as it did under Tubman's open-door years — in the absence of income redistribution, the country's wealth was concentrated in the Americo-Liberian hegemonic class. The 1980 overthrow of the ancient regime did not alter this basic structure of the Liberian economy — if anything, the situation of dependence got worse. Not only was the country in a desperate economic situation throughout the Doe years, it was pushed to a situation where foreign aid became the major foreign exchange earner for the country.[77]

---

75   The position of the United States of America was partly influenced by pressures from the Americo-Liberian dominated opposition groups.

76   For example, Baccus Matthews went ahead to contest the bye-elections organised for the vacant legislative seats the opposition parties rejected against the decision of GRANCOL. He was subsequently co-opted into the government as a minister.

77   What was really interesting was the manner in which Doe went after soliciting for aid: he always made it a condition for Liberia's friendliness with other countries and bodies.

Doe took over at the peak of austerity measures Tolbert had initiated to salvage an economy that was in very bad shape. With iron ore and rubber doing badly in the world market, the country's external debt and debt servicing ratio swelled. In 1980, total external debt was US$750 million. By 1985, the debt had doubled, with debt-servicing obligations rising from US$43 million in 1981 to US$132 million in 1986. In 1990, external debts reached an all-time high mark of US$1.4 billion. Under the circumstances, Doe had little or no alternative to depending on aid from the United States of America which he constantly described as 'our traditional friend'. In return for aid which the United States of America sometimes secured for Liberia from the IMF and World Bank, Doe committed himself to playing the role of a stooge. At one point, he ordered Libyans out of Liberia and at another, severed ties with Moscow, all in the effort to please Washington. Domestically, the United States of America tied much of the aid to the democratisation process, the continued existence of opposition parties, and the release of political detainees and prisoners. This was one of the major factors that sustained these parties, as we have already emphasised.

Between 1980 and 1986, the United States of America aids totalled US$450 million which was more than all Liberian had received in the previous 133 years. Also, up until 1987, the annual budgets depended mainly on the United States of America support. With so much reliance on the United States of America and her capitalist allies of course came greater foreign control. In 1986, the IMF, World Bank and EEC held observers at the management of the National Bank of Liberia and the Ministry of Finance. Liberia was once again, brought under international receivership as it was in the early part of the 20th Century. Similarly, in 1987, seventeen American 'operational experts' were appointed to oversee revenue collection, allocation and accounting, following the discovery by the United States of America General Accounting Office that a lot of funds previously advanced were diverted to personal use. In spite of these controls, the economy failed to improve because of gross mismanagement which was one of the grounds on which the IMF declared Liberia no longer credit-worthy in late 1986. By 1989, Doe had also fallen out of favour with the United States of America, for reasons which need not delay us here.[78] From that time till he finally fell, Doe turned to other friendly countries like South

---

78 The major reason was the refusal of the United States of America to supply military hardware to Doe.

Korea and Nigeria, whose friendship he tied closely to their being able to supply some of the country's needs.[79]

On the domestic front, the situation was equally desperate. Between 1980 and 1984, GDP declined by an annual rate of 4.4 per cent (from US$461.4 million in 1979 to US$321.6 million in 1983). Also, within the period, the economy as a whole experienced an average annual negative growth rate of nearly 5 per cent. Of course, the people were the victims of these problems. Budgets and salaries were regularly cut by as much as 25 per cent while for several months, salaries and other allowances remained unpaid to all categories of workers, including soldiers.[80] Raffle ticket sales that were never redeemed became a major source of revenue for government and new taxes — like reconstruction tax and health tax — were introduced, while people were forced to make so-called 'voluntary contributions' to country development projects, for which fund-raising ceremonies were organised. Furthermore, under a programme of structural adjustment and economic stabilisation, workers were retrenched and all forms of subsidy, except on rice were removed.[81] One cardinal principle of this programme was to attract foreign investors who had been scared away by Doe's repressive and unpredictable government. One of the incentives he introduced in pursuance of this was the amendment of the Constitution by a decree in 1985 granting foreign nationals the right to own real estate. His reason was:

> we believe that this action gives meaning and content to a real open door policy. We also urge and encourage businessmen and investors, including Lebanese, Americans and all other nationalities to come and invest here...'

Under Doe, the Liberian economy clearly became weaker and more exposed to foreign control. One mark of this control amongst Liberians at the time was the belief that only the United States of America could determine whether Doe would remain in power or not, and that any one who wanted to overthrow him had, of necessity to have American support.[82] Apart from foreign control, another important characteristic of the economy under Doe was the creation of a new class of the rich which comprised mainly African-Liberians. Like the Americo-Liberians before them, they were made

---

79   These countries supplied him weapons when the civil war eventually broke out.
80   This largely accounted for the extortionist dispositions of soldiers under Doe and also for the low morale they had during the civil war.
81   Doe was clearly guided by the experience of 1979.
82   At one stage, in 1985, many people believed Quiwonkpa had the support of the United States of America.

by the state, and their continued membership of the class depended on how loyal they were to Doe. So, the Doe years did not witness a change in the concentration of the national income in only a few hands; what they witnessed was a change in the few hands from being Americo-Liberian to being African-Liberian. As for the masses, their material conditions in fact worsened because of the economic misfortunes. Doe tried to provide amenities like housing, expanded educational opportunities, paved roads, health care facilities and radio/television national network, but these quickly decayed or proved to be only salutary.[83]

What was the implication of a poor, weak and exposed economy for inter-ethnic relations? Many studies have shown that it heightens ethnic competition and other competitions which have as their object, resource allocation through the state (Osaghae 1989; Brown 1980) Liberia did not prove to be an exception; in fact, the conflict situation was exacerbated because the major ethnic competitors were just coming out of over a century of exclusion from control of the state and the allocation of resources. This made competition for control of the state power which was and remains the open sesame to wealth and other privileges both for the elite and other groups, a stiff one. Economic immiseration only heightened it.

Against the background of the foregoing detailed outline of the major landmarks and features of the post-1980 coup period, we shall now turn to examine the situation of ethnic conflicts in that period and how it contributed to the outbreak of the civil war in 1989.

The Ethnic Situation in the Doe Years

To begin with, we should specify the relevant ethnic actors in this period. These were principally the African-Liberian groups which, on the basis of their proximity to and representation in government, as well as their activation of ethnic demands, could be classified into two categories. In the first category were those groups from which came the principal actors of the 1980 coup, who subsequently composed the PRC and other major government organs (see Tables 3 and 4). These groups were the Krahn which Doe and several other key PRC and government officials were, Gio

---

83   A first time visitor to Liberia in the Doe years would have been impressed by the giant strides in road construction, building of government ministries and departments, as well as housing estates, but these achievements were overshadowed by the corruption and repression of the government.

77

and Mano of Nimba county from which came Thomas Quiwonkpa, who many felt should have been Head of State in place of Doe, Robert Zuo and Henry Zuo; Grebo (Nicholas Podier, originally speaker of the PRC and Jerry C, Jorwley); Kru (Larry W, Borteh, Jacob Swen and Swen Dixon); Loma (Abraham Kollie and Robert Sumo) and Kissi (Fallah Varney). In terms of counties, the expanded PRC had 10 members from Grand Gedeh, 7 from Nimba, 5 from Sinue, 4 from Lofa and 1 from Bong and this, by extension, made the ethnic groups in these counties belong to this first category. Of all these groups, the main protagonists were the Krahn (Grand Gedeh) and the Gio/Mano (Nimba) who were enmeshed in conflicts throughout the Doe years. One group which belonged to this category, but not by virtue of its members being in the PRC or other key positions in government was the Mandingo group. As we saw in Chapter 1, the Mandingoes were mostly muslim merchants whose shrewdness made them the object of resentment by other indigenous groups. Mandingoes conspicuously aligned themselves with Doe to the extent that when it came to Mano/Gio — Krahn conflicts, the Mandingoes were treated as Krahn. In trying to explain this Krahn/Mandingo collaboration, the one factor that stands out very clearly is that because the Mandingoes dominated the commercial life of most hinterland counties and taxi driving in Monrovia, where they constituted a district merchant class amongst others, Doe found it expedient to align with them for the purposes of strengthening his hold on the economy.[84] Finally, from 1985 when the ban on politics was lifted, ethnic groups of the standard-bearers of the political parties became the major actors in this category. These groups were Krahn (Samuel Doe, NDPL), Gio (Jackson F, Doe, LAP), Loma (Edward Kesselly, UP) and Kissi (William Kpolleh, LUP). Again, the greatest rivalry in party terms was between Samuel Doe of NDPL and Jackson Doe of LAP, because the latter was, popularly believed to have won the 1985 election. Thus, party politics simply amounted to the continuation of Krahn — Gio/Mano conflicts by other means.

In the second category were those groups which did not have representatives in the PRC and other top organs and, after 1985, whose sons and daughters did not play prominent roles in party politics. The elite of these groups mostly aligned themselves with the main protagonists to

---

84   No other indigenous group had a concentration of wealthy merchants as the Mandingoe had.

participate in the power-sharing process. Examples of such groups are difficult, but the Vai, Gola and Gbandi came closest to them. The Americo-Liberians who were no longer conspicuous claimants to power constituted a special class within this category. Too few to assert ethnic demands as a group within (and probably because the few who did not flee the country after Doe's coup never recovered from the shock and agony they were subjected to during the coup), they nevertheless, played influential roles from outside the country. In a sense, 'they waited on the wings', and when the African-Liberians created the openings for them to return through their seemingly irreconcilable conflicts, they swooped in strongly.

The major object of political conflicts, as usual, was control of state power which determined the individual's or group's status or position and access to wealth and other privileges. The struggle, involved mainly the elites of these groups. Group consciousness and action were often mobilised on the basis of supporting Doe or Quiwonkpa. Very little of spontaneous ethnic conflicts was heard of, as these were localised within the counties and usually took the form of communal conflicts over farmland. Our concern, however, is with conflicts whose effects were national in scope and effects. These are discussed under the headings which follow.

The Issue of Krahn Domination

Quite early into his administration, Doe seemed to recognise that only through a representative power sharing formula in the composition of government, its agencies and bureaucracy, and in appointments to top military positions could a 'united Liberian' front, upon which his successful take-over of government depended, be guaranteed. This united front consisted of ethnic and non-ethnic groups, including the popular movements and remnants of the TWP. It will be seen that, at the initial stage, Doe tried to balance these groups in his appointments, though many critics felt that the appointments of former TWP leaders ran against the tide of the 'revolution'. He continually justified actions like this on the grounds of national unity, but his real motive was to neutralise or counterbalance the influence of the popular groups which tended, at that stage, to see his seizure of power as something done on their behalf. The last thing Doe would have felt comfortable with was to built his power base on radical intellectuals who could easily take over control of state affairs from him. As we have said earlier on, he was forced to declare that his government was a PRC and not a MOJA or PPP government.

Yet, it seemed so inevitable that charges of ethnic domination or ethnic injustice would ensue, considering the composition of the group of revolutionaries who staged the coup. Of the seventeen, five including Doe were Krahn. When, furthermore, in most of his earliest appointments to key positions like Director of Police and Director of Immigration, he appointed Krahns discomfort with an emerging pattern of Krahn domination was expressed. LINSU, in particular, called for a recomposition of the PRC to halt Krahn domination. The government responded by enlarging the PRC membership to 28, bringing in 9 co-members to represent other groups (see Table 4). What reinforced the fear of Krahn domination was the attitude of the Krahn people themselves. They saw in Doe's government, their own opportunity to play Americo-Liberians much to the envy of other groups and to the Gio/Mano in particular, whose son Quiwonkpa rivalled Doe in popularity. Doe took the opportunity of his nation-wide tour to reassure Liberians that his government was committed a national unity through ethnic representation in major organs of government. On one such occasion, he declared:

> Having the promotion of genuine national unity as our cardinal objective, we set up a PRC with 27 members [the 28th member was appointed later] representing all the major ethnic groups in the country. We have since maintained a cross-sectional representation of these ethnic groups in government.

In Grand Gedeh (home-county), Doe found it necessary to warn fellow Krahns who believed 'that every important position must go to them or those they favour' because he had 'observed and continue to receive reports that our own citizens are causing many problems in the nation' (Givens 1986:33). Doe was apparently referring to soldiers, many of them Krahn, who went around the counties harassing 'enemies' of the new government.[85]

Later events, particularly the coup attempts by Quiwonkpa in 1983 and 1985 and the growth of formidable anti-Doe groups both at home and abroad forced the Krahns into defence politics around Doe. At that stage, Doe no longer felt as disturbed as he was initially about allegations of Krahn domination, especially in the area of security. His personal bodyguards, executive mansion guards, State Security Services, Immigration

---

85   Liberian soldiers at the time, continuing in the LFF tradition, were notorious for harassing innocent people.

and Police were headed by and predominantly composed of Krahns. Doe also systematically built a Krahn-based army — the elite First Infantry Battalion and the Special Anti-Terrorist Unit (SATU) were almost completely Krahn. In fact, by the time the civil war broke out, it was difficult to describe the Armed Forces of Liberia as anything but Krahn army. The Krahness of the security and military forces especially made Krahn soldiers, policemen and security agents 'the guardians and bully-boys' of the political order, a fact which led Clapham (1989:109) to rightly predict that, in the event of the regime's overthrow, Krahns would be the objects of retaliation by the other groups. The Krahns did not dominate the other sectors as they did the security agencies and the army, but they were favoured and disproportionately represented enough for Doe to be accused of 'Krahness'. This was especially apparent in the contract system and ministries where the individual's ability to speak Krahn was sure to give him what he wanted. The most vocal accusations were made by the Nimba peoples for reasons which are considered below. Once, at the height of such accusations, Doe convened a world press conference to read out the names of at least 40 Gio and Mano who occupied top government positions including the Minister of Health, Agriculture and Internal Affairs, two Supreme Court Justices and Managing Director of the National Ports Authority and pointed out that all major institutions of government, including the army had top officials from Nimba county.

Krahn Vs Gio/Mano

The Krahns are the predominant group in Grand Gedeh county, while the Gio and Mano are in neighbouring Nimba county, though there is a small Krahn settlement in Nimba — the Nimba Krahn. Krahn-Mano/Gio relations date far back. Unfortunately, there has been no study of these relations (just as is the case with most other hinterland groups), but oral accounts, which are not too reliable, talk of conflicts between the two groups dating back to the early 20th Century. However long these conflicts may have been, they cannot be anywhere near those that occurred during the Doe years. When the coup that brought Doe to power took place, the Mano and Gio were as ecstatic in supporting the new government as were the Krahns; in fact, Nimba county was the first county to openly declare support for it. The reason was that there were several Gios in the new government, the most notable being Thomas Quiwonkpa who became Commanding-General of the armed forces. The assertiveness of the Krahn in claiming power generated a rivalry between them and the Gio/Mano, such that conflict between Doe and Quiwonkpa that involved little ethnic considerations easily became conflict between the two groups.

So, when Quiwonkpa organised the first coup in 1983 reprisals were unleashed on the Gio and Mano in Monrovia and in Nimba county. The anti-Doe feelings which developed in the aftermath of this was largely responsible for Doe's loss in Nimba county in the 1985 elections (the fact that Jackson Doe, Gio, was himself contesting was equally important). Matters were not helped by the widely-held belief that Jackson Doe actually won the election. From this point, the Gios and Manos became the object of victimisation in the army, bureaucracy and commerce. When Quiwonkpa struck again in November 1985 in the heat of objections by the other political parties to the election of Samuel Doe, the reprisals were even greater. This was because of the circumstances of the coup itself. The coupist seized the broadcasting house and marched through the major streets and, as they appeared to have succeeded, people took the streets in large numbers, jubilating.[86] When eventually the coup failed (Commony Wisseh, one of the coup leaders has attributed this to the intervention of Israeli security forces on the side of Doe), there were house-to-house searches for Gio and Mano in Monrovia especially because of the rumours that Quiwonkpa planned to make Jackson Doe President if he succeeded.

It can be understood then why Charles Taylor's NPFL which had all the trappings of continuity from where Quiwonkpa left off, decided to mount its insurrection from a Gio and Mano springboard, as we shall discuss in Chapter 5.

The Americo-Liberians

Although they had been displaced, the Americo-Liberians remained critical actors in the struggle for the control of state power. Following the coup, most of them fled abroad, taking with them the country's technocratic power whose absence, all through, threatened the performance of Doe's government in virtually every sector. At several points, Doe made passionate appeals to them to return home to no avail. The few who remained (including those who returned) continued to enjoy privileges from the state, including appointments to plum ministerial (Eastman was Foreign Affairs Minister for a long time) and other important positions

---

86   This was ample evidence of the increased unpopularity of Doe.

(Chairmanship of SECOM and Directorship of National Bank of Liberia). What was interesting was that, in terms of political affiliation, no Americo-Liberian based political party existed and furthermore, a good number of those who decided to participate in party politics belonged to the NDPL.

The main basis of Americo-Liberian oppositional politics however lay abroad, especially the United States of America, where they formed several Liberian associations in alliance with African-Liberians who also fled from Doe's repression. These associations, as has been pointed out earlier pursued their interests through seeking to influence the United States of America's official policy towards Doe. It was in recognition of the powerful influence they had in this regard that Doe tried at several points to curry their favour. When the civil war broke out, he found it necessary to send a delegation led by an Americo-Liberian to the United States of America to explain his government's position to the Liberian associations and other influential caucuses.

5 - The Civil War

In this chapter, we examine the highest point of conflicts so far reached in Liberia, namely, the civil war that erupted on December 24, 1989. In the process of state-building, as we saw in Chapter 2, there were several cases of violent conflicts between the settlers and the indigenes and among the indigenes themselves. From the Tubman years, however, the incidence of violent conflicts, especially those which involved the brutal force of the LFF reduced tremendously, largely because Americo-Liberian hegemonic rule had been consolidated. This was the transition phase from conquest to incorporation (and assimilation) which required less violence. Then came the late 1970s when economic hardships finally provided the basis for opposition groups to mobilise African-Liberians against the Americo-Liberian oligarchy that had monopolised power since 1847. This created the enabling environment for the violent overthrow of the old regime in the coup d'etat of 12 April 1980. The aftermath of that coup saw Doe unleashing a reign on terror and violent politics such as the country had never experienced. But none of these previous experiences with violent conflicts came anywhere near the civil war which is devastating the country.

Not many scholars would be surprised that the war broke out, given the history of the country. It can be regarded as an inevitable consequence of the military character of the Liberian state from the very beginning which Doe carried to the limits (See Chapter 2). This character made violent overthrow the most viable approach to ending Americo-Liberian hegemonic rule in 1980 (Givens 1986) and Doe's rule. In the latter case, not only was it impossible to oust Doe by democratic means, it was also difficult to do so from within Liberia itself, as the 'invasion' character of Quiwonkpa's coups and Charles Taylor's uprising vividly show.[87] The significance of the civil war however went beyond being a consequence of the militarism of the state. It was also an inevitable consequence of the larger crisis of the Liberian state which was bound to come to a head sooner or later. The manifestations of this crisis are well known: the exclusion of the majority African-Liberians who constituted only about 2.0 per cent of the total population for over a century; the class contradictions which saw less than 1 per cent of the country's population enjoying about 70 per cent of the

---

87   The point is that Doe had a complex security network which made it difficult for plans to be hatched within.

nation's wealth, a situation MOJA's slogan described as 'Monkey Work, Baboon Draw'; a weak, exposed and dependent economy whose control was almost completely in foreign hands; the state was the only means of social reproduction; the state was frequently in decay, as political structures could never prevent personal rule or guarantee human liberty and political participation; etc. If these aspects of the crisis were attributed to Americo-Liberian hegemonic rule, Doe proved that they were not a function of the group that ruled really, and that such attributions were wrong. Indeed, the national crisis worsened under Doe and it is not surprising that the civil war erupted in his time. Those African-Liberians who welcomed him as their liberator from colonial rule in 1980 certainly needed a second independence which was what Taylor's movement at the beginning seemed to promise. What is interesting here is that independence appeared to be all that mattered, not whether it was led by Taylor, an Americo-Liberian or Moses Duopu, a Gio. But was this really so?

In saying that the civil war was inevitable, the suggestion is not that the Liberian crisis could only be resolved violently. Rather, it is that by closing other alternatives, Doe (and his predecessors) made non-violent change impossible. But whether violent or non-violent indications had been there all along that Liberia would some day erupt, and many thought by 1980 that the eruption had taken place. Doe's inability to bring about desirable changes, especially in the area of making control of state power the exclusive preserve of only one person, or a few families and one ethnic group, simply postponed the eruption day until the civil war.

Several more questions are raised by the war itself. What was its real character? As the catharsis of the Liberian crisis, was it an ethnic or class or religious war, or simply a matter of personal greed written large? Or a complex combination of these? What were the stakes of the war? What was the overall effect of the war on the ethnic situation, and what does the future look like? To be able to answer questions like these properly, we need to first re-examine the transformed terrain of ethnic politics which provides a necessary background to understanding the actors and stakes of the civil war.

The Transformed Terrain of Ethnic Politics: A Resume

Up until 1980, the political division in Liberia was still essentially between the Americo-Liberians and the African-Liberians, as they corresponded to the ruling and oppressed classes respectively. The assimilation of African-Liberian elite did not change the cleavage lines because of the hegemonic character of Americo-Liberian domination. The dominated classes on the other hand, were almost exclusively African-Liberian and, in relation to the Americo-Liberians, they presented a united front. The only incipient cleavage with potentials for political relevance in a Liberia free of ethclass hegemonic rule at the time was that .between the hinterland (the up-country) peoples and the coastal peoples. The latter considered themselves next to the Americo-Liberians in the socio-political hierarchy having been incorporated into Liberia from the very beginning.[88] Their elite formed the vast majority of the assimilated African-Liberians, and were clearly favoured by the Americo-Liberians in appointments to government positions. The upcountry folks, on the other hand, were fully incorporated into Liberia only in the 1960s, and continued to be looked down upon both by the Americo-Liberians and the coastland African-Liberians. The entry of their elites into the privileged classes was slow and laborious, and it was not until 1973 that the first upcountry ministers were appointed. The preponderance of 'upcountry boys' in the 1980 coup summarily silenced the coastal peoples whose elite had identified more with the Americo-Liberians than African-Liberians (of the hinterland). Doe's government continued to be dominated by elements from the hinterland and, it is not surprising that when division came within African-Liberian ranks, it did not follow the hinterland coastal lines. It is very likely that if Americo-Liberian domination had been terminated through democratic means, the hinterland-coastal cleavage would have featured more prominently. This is still a possibility in post-civil war Liberia, particularly because the numerically disadvantaged Americo-Liberians may most likely forge an alliance with the coastlanders, now that the upcountry boys have 'misused their opportunity'.[89]

The 1980 coup and its aftermath transformed the ethnic scenario in significant ways that altered the political configuration among the groups. The most dramatic of these related to the Americo-Liberians who were displaced from the privileged position of being the mainstay of the ruling class, but not from the class itself. In other words, in the manner of the circulation of elites, Americo-Liberians were displayed from the governing elite position and pushed to that of the non-governing elite. As such, they remained critical actors in the competition for the control of state power. Two important points clearly distinguished their new form of competition.

---

88   Evidence of such feelings can still be found in Liberia today.
89   This view was expressed by an Americo-Liberian student of mine way back in 1989.

First, much of it took the form of opposition to Doe and was organised from abroad especially the United States of America where most of them fled after the 1980 coup. The organisational basis for this opposition was provided by the various interest and pressure groups like the Association for Constitutional Democracy in Liberia (ACDL) and the Association of Liberians in the United States of America. Although these groups were not exclusively Americo-Liberian in membership, their leadership and activities were directed by them. They organised symposia, demonstrations and made representations to both the Congress and the State Department as part of their efforts to influence the United States of America policy towards Liberia in ways that best served their interests. In an interview, Amos Sawyer revealed that the main work of the ACDL, which he led involved lobbying the United States of America Congress and providing information to newspapers and other agencies on the Liberian situation (*West Africa*, 7 October, 1990). These groups were in the forefront of making the release of political detainees and prisoners as well as return to civil rule conditions for the United States of America aid to Liberia. Doe recognised the critical positions of the Americo-Liberians in the United States of America on their support to his government. Consequently, he made several attempts to incorporate them into his government. He not only offered the olive branch and asked them to return to Liberia, he also appointed them to top and sensitive positions: Emmet Harmon was made SECOM Chairman, while Winston Tubman was appointed to the strategic position of Liberian Representative at the United Nations.

Although these overtures were constantly rebuffed because Doe refused to change his repressive character, he persisted in sending delegations to the United States of America to woo Americo-Liberians leaders and black congressional caucuses at points of crisis when there was formidable opposition at home. The high point of this strategy was in April 1990 at the height of the civil war when Doe sent a high-powered government delegation to the United States of America to negotiate ways in which the NPFL's battle against him could be brought to an end. He perceived that Taylor's 'rebellion' was at the behest of the Americo-Liberian groups, and was therefore, willing to meet conditions laid down by them. These included a restoration of diplomatic ties with the United States of America, granting general amnesty to political prisoners, lifting the ban on political associations like Sawyer's LPP, bringing forward the elections scheduled for 1991 to some time earlier and a guarantee from Doe that he would no longer take part in the presidential election.[90] Although conceding these grounds were not sufficient to stop Taylor, the overall point is that the Americo-Liberians still wielded enormous power, using their strong connections in the United States of America (and elsewhere). In fact, by the time the civil war broke out, they emerged not only as power brokers but, more importantly, as king-makers.

The second important point about the transformed character of Americo-Liberians competition for power was that with the loss of its hegemonic control, the group because of its size, was no longer in a position to compete alone. In other words, having lost its control over the African-Liberian elite and now having to compete freely and equally with them, the Americo-Liberian group lacked the numerical strength to compete alone. Moreover, their operation from outside Liberia made such competition difficult, if not impossible. These factors made it more or less compulsory for them to forge alliances with African-Liberians, especially the disenchanted and opposition elements amongst them, and brought them into alliance politics for which they became famous in the Doe years and during the civil war. They aligned with African-Liberian exiles who also fled from Doe's tyrannical rule, some of whom formed inclusive associations like the Council of Nimba Citizens in the United States of America, while others belonged to groups like the ACDL which, as we have pointed out, had Americo-Liberian leadership. It was from one of such groups, the Union of Liberian Associations in the United States of America which had a large African-Liberian membership, that Charles Taylor's NPFL drew its major support (Sawyer 1990). Alliances based in the United States of America and elsewhere could not however, be effective if they were not also established within Liberia itself. Outlets were found in the opposition parties and coupists like Quiwonkpa who were known to enjoy moral and material support from Liberians outside.[91] Along the same lines, it is interesting to know that the roots of Charles Taylor's NPFL are traced to Quiwonkpa's earlier attempts to overthrow Doe and that the Front had

---

90 Although he made these concessions, Doe was not willing to negotiate with Charles Taylor whom he continuously referred to as 'a criminal'.

91 Shortly before he organised the November 1985 coup, Quiwonkpa was in the United States of America, and it is not unlikely that it was from there he got the encouragement to try again.

the character of an Americo-Liberian/African-Liberian alliance from the beginning.

The transformations within the African-Liberian segment of the ethnic terrain were even more dramatic. This segment which had hitherto presented a united front vis-à-vis the Americo-Liberians disintegrated. This disintegration did not however, follow the hinterland-coastal peoples cleavage which political developments in the country had accentuated, for reasons already explained (See p.86-88). Instead, it involved 'upcountry' elements, principally, the Gio and Mano of Nimba county (the Mandingoes were also concentrated in Nimba) and the Krahn of Grand Gedeh. This was because the new ruling class was dominated by upcountry elites in the army, cabinet, bureaucracy, university and fledging private sector. The major character of this new class was that it was a factionalised rather than a hegemonic class, a factional system being one in which there is a narrow political arena and in which the elite is fragmented along ethnic lines and where a high value is placed on personal power (Nicholson 1972; Brass 1965). Factional politics heightened the competition for control of state power and, because Doe greatly reduced the scope of opposition groups to function, they were willing allies of foreign-based opposition groups.

One of the bases for factionalisation which became prominent in the aftermath of the 1980 coup was christian/muslim division. As pointed out in Chapter 1, Liberia has been referred to all along as a christian country, but this was only because christianity was a mark of Americo-Liberian hegemony as, in reality, there were more muslims (and traditional religionists) than christians in the country. The ascendancy of African-Liberian elites, therefore, provided the opportunity for muslim elites to insist on an official recognition of their presence in the country. The task of doing this fell principally on the Mandingoes, and, although they did not quite succeed in changing the continued reference to the country as a christian state, there was ample evidence in the media and official communications that the presence of Islam, had been established.[92] It took the civil war, finally, to complete this process. During the war, muslims, the bulk of whom were Mandingoes in Nimba county were persecuted by the NPFL:

---

92   For example, on Fridays, Muslim programmes were aired on television and radio, just as Christian programmes were on Sundays.

89

mosques were forcibly closed down in all NPFL controlled areas until July 1991, and many people were killed simply because they were muslims.[93] It was in response to this that the Movement for the Redemption of Liberian Muslims was formed in 1990 in Conakry, Guinea. The movement later joined forces with other pro-Doe militarised groups to form ULIMO whose agenda consisted of protecting the integrity of muslims, Krahns and Mandingoes, and preventing Charles Taylor from achieving his ambition to rule the country. Muslims have, through the war, brought themselves to the position where discussions of peace in post-War Liberia have Christian-Muslim balance as one of the mechanisms for bringing about peace and stability (Moniba 1992).

The non-elite, particularly those of the hinterland counties who were fully participating in the political system for the first time were mobilised along factional lines by the elite. The activities of ethnic associations whose members were drawn from urban workers and masses were stepped up in support of the elite. Again, this was truest of the Krahn, Gio and Mano and Mandingo, whose associations in Monrovia were used to mobilise ethnic support. As we have seen in the case of the Association of Nimba citizens in the United States of America, such associations were also formed outside the country.[94] These associations did not however, only function as instruments of ethnic conflicts as determined by the elite. They continued in their 'traditional' roles of meeting members' welfare needs, contributing to the developments of their home areas and engaging in non-elite ethnicity. Non-elite ethnicity usually takes the form of the worker, market woman, student and other non-elites furthering their individual and collective interests by using the elite, usually those in government (Osaghae 1991).

One way of summarising all these is to say that the Doe years and the civil war provided the opportunity for all aspects of the Liberian conflict situation, including those like religion that had remained latent all along, to be given vent. With all the transformations that we have analysed, how do we begin to characterise the ethnic terrain in the Doe years and situate the civil war within it? Was the Americo-Liberian/African-Liberian cleavage still critical, for example? From what has been said, it became only one of the critical cleavages not because the Americo-Liberians no longer existed

---

93   This claim by Alhaji Kromah should be taken as applying to the Mandingoes (and the Krahn Muslims) rather than the Gio Vai or other Muslims.

94   This facilitated cross-ethnic alliances with Americo-Liberian groups.

as a self-perpetuating group (intermarriage with other Liberians is still unpopular, for example, and clear Americo-Liberian under-currents have featured prominently in the civil war)[95] but because having lost control of state power, Americo-Liberians have found it impossible to operate alone in the renewed struggle for it (the more so formations that this struggle has, in the main, involved African-Liberian groups). Their subsequent alliance with African-Liberian individuals and groups (to oust Doe and return to power possibly) renders any discussion of purely Americo-Liberian actions difficult but, at the same time, it does not mean that the basic cleavage has been broken. What can be said is that alliance and collaborative politics have afforded the opportunity for new class structures to be forged between elites of the two groups on relatively equalitarian terms, rather than on terms set by Americo-Liberians as was the case during the era of hegemonic rule.[96] This process has involved factional intra-class struggles which manifest in the civil war as accusations by some African-Liberian elites that the Americo-Liberians exploited the circumstances of the civil war to attempt to recreate the old order. But Americo-Liberian/African-Liberian cleavage had become only one of the critical cleavages; the other critical ones which were prominent in the civil war were intra-African-Liberian ethnicity, particularly between the Gio and Mano on the one hand, and the Krahn and Mandingo on the other; factional politics and, to some extent, religion.

Let us now turn to examine the civil war itself. It is only after we have done this that we can be in a position to determine how much of the civil war can be discussed in ethnic terms.

The Course of the Civil War

There are several dimensions to the civil war, and except we clearly delineate the scope and boundaries of our concern, we run the risk of pursuing an unmanageable exploration. In terms of the major participants in the war, is it correct to regard the war as involving only the Krahn, Gio, Mano, Mandingo and Americo-Liberians? At the beginning, most Liberians thought the crisis was a replay of Quiwonkpa's previous attempts to seize

---

95   These have taken the form of allegations of Americo-Liberian arrogance by Taylor.
96   The Americo-Liberians nevertheless retain the advantage of having greater resources.

power, and that it involved only these groups,[97] but by the time it erupted into a full-scale war, all Liberians became involved. In fact, negotiations and conferences held to find solutions to the crisis provided ample opportunity for the other groups to carve out respectable places for themselves in the power sharing process. The emergence of several groups in the course of the war enhanced this development even though, the actual process of fighting involved mainly the Krahns, Mandingo, Gio, Mano and Americo-Liberians. Groups like the Kpelle and Loma whose members were preponderant in the Armed Forces of Liberia (AFL) ante-civil war increasingly found themselves sidelined when the army became an instrument of Krahn struggle.

In terms of the factors that precipitated the war, its locations within a national crisis whose roots lie in the very foundation of the country, means that the scope of the war goes far back in time than the actual period when it took place. The previous chapters of this study have fortunately dealt with aspects of this crisis from 1820 to the immediate pre-civil war years. We shall therefore, concentrate more on the immediate factors of the civil war (against the backdrop of the past). Another issue requiring delineation relates to the national and international dimensions of the war. To many observers, the war is prominent because of the international character it had from the beginning: Taylor's NPFL soldiers were trained in Libya whose leader, Colonel Gadaffi had a score to settle with Doe;[98] the NPFL at the beginning comprised several non-Liberians particularly from Burkina Faso; Taylor attacked through Cote d'Ivoire with the backing of Libya and Burkina Faso; ECOWAS intervened in the war through its Monitoring group (ECOMOG) which at a stage actually fought in the war; the United States of America has been involved in diverse ways;[99] etc. For these reasons, it is difficult to separate the internal from the international dimensions of the war but the war remained principally a Liberian war. Our focus is therefore on the internal dimensions on the crisis and the international dimensions will be examined only to the extent that they help

---

97 This was why many residents of Monrovia waited until the last minute before fleeing from the war.

98 Doe was initially quite close to Gadaffi but fell out with him in spite of Libya's great investments in Liberia to please his American benefactors.

99 Shortly before ECOMOG was formed, most Liberians both at home and abroad demanded American intervention to end the crisis. But she has done over the years, the United States of America refused to intervene.

to clarify issues. We outline below the principal actors in the war, and the partisan characters they presented.

Charles Taylor's NPFL

According to one account, the NPFL was co-founded by Moses Duopu and Charles Taylor whose initial position was head of the military section, (Johnson 1990). The exact date when the NPFL emerged is not known. Indications are that its origins may lie in attempts to continue or exploit the struggle initiated by Quiwonkpa. This is most probable when it is considered that, apart from Americo-Liberians like Charles Taylor, and Earnest Eastman, the other leaders of the NPFL — Moses Duopu, Tom Woewiyu and David Duayon — were Gio from Nimba county. Moreover, utterances by Taylor himself sometimes suggested a continuity between Quiwonkpa's movement and his NPFL which were both based on a Gio/Mano/Nimba support base.[100] In terms of this support base, what is certain is that notwithstanding the prominence of Gio elite in the NPFL, the Front exploited the existing conflict situation between the Gio/Mano and the Krahn/Mandingo. In fact, the guerrilla force that the NPFL used to attack with originally was significantly non-Liberian. It was only after Doe's Krahn soldiers had responded to the NPFL's incursion which they perceived as a continuation of the battle started by Quiwonkpa and which led them to massacre Gios and Manos and sack whole villages in Nimba county that the Gios and Manos were forced to join forces with the NPFL. It is wrong therefore, to define the NPFL as a Mano and Gio movement — in fact, it was the unease some Gios felt over the trend of Taylor's killing of prominent NPFL leaders (who were Gios coincidentally?) that provided the grounds for Prince Johnson to break away and receive ample support from Gio soldiers to form the INPFL.

The NPFL was founded in the United States of America where Charles Taylor had fled in 1985 and was serving a jail term on charges of embezzling about US$1 million when he served as Director of General Service Agency under Doe.[101] Support was recruited for the formation of the NPFL amongst the various associations of Liberians in the United States

---

100 For example, when he announced the re-opening of mosques in Nimba county, Taylor said he and the Gios and Manos 'really came to liberate Liberians from Doe's oppression and not to revenge' (*West Africa*, 28 July 1991).

101 The story is that he broke jail to launch his rebel attack.

ot America and Americo-Liberian groups in particular were known to provide moral and financial support. Whatever the origins of the NPFL may have been, Charles Taylor has, through a systematic elimination of other claimants to leadership, emerged as the essence of the Front. In fact, the Front has been described as a one-man band which has no 'central committee or politburo, no political manifesto or party programme. Taylor... .akes all the major decisions himself' (*Africa Confidential*, 27 July 1990:5). Once this character of the NPFL became known, many leaders like Amos Sawyer and Ellen Johnson — Sirleaf withdrew the support they previously gave it because they saw Taylor's ambition only leading to the replacement of one dictatorship by another. The aim of NPFL was to flush Doe out of power and take over control of the government with Charles Taylor as President. It is possible that if Doe's soldiers did not unwittingly force the Nimba peoples into supporting Taylor, the country would have been spared the civil war. But, after they had been forced to join the NPFL, apart from Taylor's ambition, the NPFL's sub-agenda became to revenge against the Krahn and their Mandingo collaborators.

Prince Johnson's INPFL

Prince Johnson, a Gio, is a commissioned officer of the AFL who rose to become Commander of the Liberian military police in 1976. Later, he joined forces with Charles Taylor's NPFL and, after receiving his training on guerrilla warfare in Libya, was made Commander of the NPFL army after the death of Elmer Johnson, the former Commander. In July 1990, he broke away from the Independent National Patriotic Front of Liberia (NPFL) along with several hundred Gio and Mano 'commandos' to form the INPFL on the grounds of anti-African-Liberian actions pursued by Taylor. According to Johnson himself, he broke away because: 'the indigenous members of NPFL were being treated like fools. We were only being asked to go and fight without being taken into confidence about other details'. Continuing, he said that after Duopu and other Nimba leaders had been killed; 'we reasoned that gradually, the Congoes are going to use us again as pawns. We therefore decided to do something, before it is too late for us' (Johnson 1990).

Like the NPFL, the INPFL's target was ousting Doe, and, in the process of doing this, the Krahn and Mandingoes were the objects of attack. In September 1990, Johnson and his men captured Doe at the headquarters of the ECOMOG and subsequently killed him. The act made Johnson a prominent actor in the crisis and the INPFL became part of the search for peace on the side of ECOMOG and the interim government. It is difficult to ascertain the actual character of Johnson's INPFL because of the unpredictable and indiscriminate nature of its killings and other operations. Even though it was predominantly Gio and Mano, commandos from these groups were constantly executed on the orders of Johnson. Nevertheless, based on its major objects of attack and Johnson's statements, the INPFL's fight was against Krahns, Mandingoes and Americo-Liberians.

The AFL

Under Doe, the AFL was transformed from its previous multiethnic composition into an instrument for protecting his rule and the domination of Krahns. It became Krahn-dominated, and this was particularly true of the Special Anti-Terrorist Unit (SATU) and the First Battalion, the two major units of the army which by 1988 were the only armed units (apart from the Executive Mansion Guard which was also Krahn-dominated). When Taylor struck first at Butuo in Nimba county, Doe sent predominantly Krahn soldiers to 'arrest' the situation. Following the pattern already established in 1983 and 1985, these soldiers sacked villages in Nimba county, killing and maiming hundreds of them. It was this unfortunate response by Doe that pushed the Nimba peoples into supporting the NPFL. When a full-scale war erupted, Doe found that, increasingly, only soldiers who were Krahn could be trusted. In May 1990, Gio and Mano soldiers in the army were disarmed, clamped in detention, or killed. Thereafter, only Krahn were made Commandos and it was the alienation of soldiers from other groups like Kpelle and Loma and the collapse of the country's economy which left soldiers in several months arrears of salaries that weakened Doe's resistance to rebel attacks.[102] After Doe was killed, the AFL continued to function as a 'Krahn army' until many Krahn soldiers defected to ULIMO and the interim government of Amos Sawyer undertook to reorganise it.

ULIMO

ULIMO was formed in June 1991 as a conglomeration of independent fighting groups whose basis for coming together was that they all formally

---

102 By the end of May 1990, things were so bad that government was forced to direct all hotels in the country to turn in all foreign currency in their possession.

supported Doe and were either committed to avenging his death, or preventing Taylor (and Americo-Liberians) from entering power, or negotiating better places for their groups in post-civil war Liberia. Two groups representing these independent forces came together to form ULIMO. These groups were the Movement for the Redemption of Liberian Muslims which was predominantly made up of Mandingoes who had fled to Guinea and was led by Alhaji G. Kromah who served as Director of the National Broadcasting Services in the Doe regime; and the Liberian United Defence Force, which was predominantly Krahn and led by William Glay, George Boley, Abraham Kollie, Raleigh Seekie, George Toe Washington and General Karpeh, all Krahn except for Abraham who is Loma. Although, ULIMO described itself as 'a non-tribal, non-sectarian organisation born out of the desire of displaced Liberians to return home and continue their search for democratic freedom' and had, as its main objective, the redemption of Liberians from the terrorism of Taylor (*West Africa*, 28 July, 1991) it was basically the Krahn/Mandingo/Muslim United Front in the war after 1990. Its major activity was fighting the NPFL from its Sierra-Leonian base, and its future was constantly threatened by factional politics among its elite which resulted in the murder of General Karpeh, its military commander in May 1992.

Highlights of Events During the War

October 1989: First hints of NPFL's attack. A village chief in Nimba county reported to the President about strange movements involving military activities in the county. A panel headed by the Minister of Internal Affairs, himself from Nimba county, was set up to investigate. The panel reported that the Superintendent's information was false alarm.

December 1989: On the 24th, Charles Taylor's NPFL advanced into Butuo, Nimba county, from Cote d'Ivoire.

January 1990: Doe sent about 500 AFL soldiers, mostly Krahn, under the command of Brigadier-General Edward Smith into Nimba county to 'arrest the rebel incursion'. The soldiers massacred hundreds of Gios and Manos with the assistance of Mandingo informants.

April 1990: Doe sent a delegation to the United States of America led by Winston Tubman on a fence-mending mission with United States of America-based opposition groups which were believed to be behind Taylor. Many members of the delegation seized the opportunity to flee the country.

May 1990: The United Nations premises in Sinkor, Monrovia, was invaded by Doe's soldiers who went in search of Gios and Manos taking refuge there (since January several of them had been killed, and the killings were stepped up each time there were reports of NPFL victory in the war).

-----------Doe issued a two-week ultimatum to Charles Taylor, failing which he threatened to wipe out Nimba county completely and declare total war.

-----------The ECOWAS Summit at Banjul, Gambia set up a mediation Committee to seek ways of ending the crisis.

July 1990: Government troops killed over 200 Mano and Gio, mostly women and children who were taking refuge in St. Peter's Lutheran Church in Monrovia under the auspices of the Red Cross.

-----------Prince Johnson broke away from the NPFL to form the INPFL.

-----------Taylor announced the formation of the National Patriotic Assembly of Reconciliation and declared himself President of Liberia.

August 1990: The ECOWAS decided to send a Monitoring Group (ECOMOG) comprising soldiers from Nigeria, Ghana, Sierra Leone, Guinea and Gambia (this was later enlarged to include soldiers from Senegal) to Liberia. The mandate given to ECOMOG included effecting a cease-fire, setting up an interim government and conducting fresh election. Charles Taylor opposed ECOMOG from the very beginning.

-----------As part of its peace-making initiatives, the all-Liberia conference organised under the auspices of ECOWAS was held in Banjul, Gambia. The conference which was attended by representatives of the warring parties including the government, political parties and other organised associations, including the Teachers Association elected an interim government headed by Professor Amos Sawyer and consisting also of an interim National Assembly. Both Doe and Taylor rejected this:

September 1990: On the 9th, Doe was captured by Prince Johnson and his men at the ECOMOG headquarters at Bushrod Island, and subsequently killed.

September - December 1990: Serious fighting between the NPFL on the one hand, and the ECOMOG/AFL on the other. Taylor's NPFL was pushed out of Monrovia, and subsequently established a separate government with headquarters in Gbarnga, thereby, bringing the country under two administrations: one at Gbarnga and the other at Monrovia. This dualisation continued throughout the period of the crisis and it is difficult to tell what its long-run effects will be.

November 1990: At an extra-ordinary summit of ECOWAS leaders held in Bamako, Mali, the warring factions signed a cease-fire agreement.

------------Amos Sawyer finally moved into Monrovia from Sierra-Leone where he had been temporarily operating from. He was sworn in as interim President, and immediately assumed duty from the Ducor Palace Hotel.

January - December 1991: The gulf between Taylor and the interim government widened. Taylor remained intransigent over peace proposals proffered by ECOWAS leaders at Yamussukro, Cote d'Ivoire. It was under the circumstances that ULIMO emerged.

Situating and Interpreting the War

How is the civil war to be explained and how much of this can be ethnic? We have seen that the main combatants had discernible ethclass characters and that their battles were directed against specific groups. Is this sufficient ground to conclude that the war was ethnic, or was it a classical case of a factionalised elite mobilising the ethnic resource to mask selfish class and personal interests and ambitions? In other words, was ethnicity an independent variable *ab initio* or, was it invoked to rationalised and engender personal and intra-class struggles for power? To be sure, several interpretations of the war have been given and, although they tend to be tentative, speculatory or unsubstantiated, most of them agree that the factors which precipitated the war lie in the country's long-drawn history, a point which we made earlier on. It is in terms of the immediate factors for the war and the course of the war itself, that interpretations differ. Before we can conclude on the actual character of the war, we need to critically examine some of the popular interpretations that have been given.

One interpretation sees the war as a consequence of the high content of foreign involvement and control in Liberian affairs: Doe was a stooge of the United States of America which supported him in spite of his atrocities, but decided to ditch him when he became too unpopular: Taylor was used by Gadaffi (Libya); Houphouet Boigny (Cote d'Ivoire) and Blaise Campaore (Burkina Faso) to settle old scores with Doe; Johnson was 'planted' by the United States of America to break the backbone of Taylor whom it could not trust and to eliminate Doe; the involvement of West African leaders complicated the civil war. The problem with this kind of interpretation is that it transfers the locus of the war to the international arena, thereby glossing over or actually undermining the critical factors making for the war within the country itself. There is no doubt that external forces played a significant part in the crisis leading up to the war and the war itself, but these should be seen as facilitating factors engendered by the combatants themselves in furtherance of their objectives. As was the case with other civil wars in Africa — Chad, Nigeria, Uganda, Rwanda, Somalia and Congo — external involvement is only one of the means of fighting internal wars in neo-colonial peripheral states.

Another interpretation situates the war within the framework of the global democratisation revolution of the 1980s which in Africa took the form of liberation from dictatorial regimes or what has been called the 'second independence movements' (Joseph 1991). As it were, the 'first independence' failed to fulfil the promises of the struggles for it because dictatorships, corrupt governments and economic mismanagement were installed. In particular, democratic channels for popular participation or through which unpopular leaders could be removed either did not exist or, where they did, they were merely cosmetic. Liberia had more than a fair share of the experience for African-Liberians who had been excluded from the political mainstream for over a century. Doe failed them woefully to the extent that some Liberians recalled the days of Americo-Liberian hegemonic rule with nostalgia.[103] Along these lines, the Liberian war has been interpreted as having been instigated by the resolve to end Doe's dictatorial, high handed and corrupt government and install a democratic regime. For example, a conference on the process of reconciliation and unity in Liberia

---

103   Several Liberian workers I talked to at the University of Liberia had such sentiments.

organised by the Association of Liberians in the United States of America at the University of Pennsylvania in January 1991, attributed the war to the acquiescent and corrupt practices of the Doe regime. Indeed, it was the anti-dictatorial motives initially read into Taylor's efforts that accounted for his being given ample support by the United States of America-based Liberian associations. This support was withdrawn once they found out Taylor's real agenda which showed him as a personal dictator, and this fact in part, helps to explain why the war did not end after Doe was killed, as many predicted.[104]

The real strength of this interpretation lies in two facts. The first is that it helps to explain why it was possible to have a coalition of forces committed to removing Doe from power. The second is that it enables us to understand why the overthrow of Doe was violent: Doe had closed the doors of non-violent replacement. As Sawyer (1990) put it in an interview:

> I must say honestly that many Liberians by the beginning of 1989 had become convinced that there was no legal recourse, and perhaps some extra-legal measures such as the use of force was the only way to get a new start in the Liberian scene.

Notwithstanding, the suggestion that Taylor's (or Johnson's, or even ULIMO's) objective was democratisation which is implicit in the interpretation is not valid, in part, because, as has already been emphasised, Taylor's ambition was simply to become President of Liberia at all costs. The other problem with this interpretation is that by grouping anti-Doe and pro-democracy forces together, it does not enable us to see the actual character of the groups involved in the struggle.

Which brings us to the interpretations that relate to the ethnic dimensions of the crisis. One of these is that Taylor and his collaborators had the objective of returning the Americo-Liberians to their position of governing elite. This view owes a lot to the fact that Charles Taylor is himself Americo-Liberian, that he had ample support from Americo-Liberian elites, a development which Prince Johnson saw as preparing the grounds for Americo-Liberian domination. Doe himself read Americo-Liberian motives behind Taylor's rebel movement, which was why he sent a delegation to the United States of America to negotiate with them. But, while he did this, his AFL soldiers descended on American-Liberians in Monrovia and Caresburg.

---

104   After Doe was killed, the new fight was stopping Taylor from becoming President of Liberia.

These pointers are mostly conjectural and, even if they are not, they do not provide sufficient grounds for asserting that the war was precipitated by an attempt by Americo-Liberians through Taylor to re-establish the old order. For one thing, Taylor was interested only in being President of Liberia[105] and, to do this, he was prepared to use Americo-Liberians and African-Liberians; anyone who stood in his way whether Americo or African-Liberian was eliminated (inside accounts say, for example, that he arranged the death of Elmer Johnson, fellow Americo-Liberian whom he saw as a rival claimant to power). The only thing that can be said is that since the 1980 coup, the Americo-Liberians had always looked forward to an opportunity which could enable them to work themselves back to respectable places in the power-sharing process. That opportunity finally came as a result of the war.

The other interpretation is that the war was simply another extreme instance of 'tribal warfare' for which newly independent African states are well known. This is based on the fact that it was a war which pitched the Gio/Mano/Americo-Liberians against the Krahn/Mandingo/Muslims. From all that has been said above, this is a misleading interpretation. First, the ethnic factor was a dependent variable as it was mobilised to personal ends by Taylor's NPFL and Doe. It was, as we have said, a classical case of elite-directed ethnicity in which the masses become falsely conscious (Mafeje 1971): underneath the veil of ethnic survival and struggles lay clear personal and class interests on the part of a factionalised elite represented by Doe, Taylor, Johnson, Duopu, Kromah, Eastman, Woewiyu and others. Second, the ethnic argument cannot explain the high non-Liberian (Burkinabe, especially) content of Taylor's NPFL, and the terror unleashed on ordinary Gios and Manos by these mercenary soldiers. Third, if the war is restricted only to the Gio, Mano, Krahn, Mandingo and Americo-Liberians, then it would be difficult to explain the killings of several other Liberians, particularly elites like Dr. Stephen Yekeson (Gbandi), Gabriel William Kpolleh (Kpelle), Chea S. Kayee (Grebo), Larry Borteh (Kru) and Fred Blay (Kru). Finally, to interpret it in terms of a 'tribal warfare' is to shield over the role of Americo-Liberians in the war.

What emerges from all this is that the war only had the appearance of ethnic warfare; it was really a personal/factionalised elite struggle which

---

105 But there can never be anything near their old hegemonic rule, and this is the lastir importance of the 1980 coup.

resulted from Taylor's selfish ambition to come into power by all means and, conversely, Doe's unwillingness to leave power. These two extreme positions determined the course of the war as the two men mobilised the ethnic resource to further their interests. All other elites defined themselves within the two extremes, leaving in the middle, Americo-Liberian elites who brokered the internal peace process and who appear to be the major beneficiaries in post-War Liberia.

6 - Conclusions

In this study, we have examined the unique ethnic situation in Liberian in historical perspective, and have analysed how much of the political realities and conflicts can be explained in terms of ethnicity. The first problem that besets an endeavour like this which we devoted Chapter 1 and substantial parts of subsequent chapters to is how to conceptualise of the ethnic situation in the face of major transformations that have taken place in the ethnic terrain over the years. Historically, conflict situations in Liberia have involved two sets of cleavages which scholars have often located separately but which, we insisted, require to be integrated if the situation both in the past and present is to be properly understood. On the one hand are the African-Liberian groups which meet all the criteria for defining ethnic groups in Africa-language, myth of common descent, core-territoriality and in-group/out-group consciousness — and whose political behaviour could be analysed in ethnic terms. On the other hand, are the Americo-Liberians who do not possess the primordial character of African ethnic groups — no vernacular language, no indigenous culture, no myth of common descent and so on — and who are best likened to white settlers in South Africa and elsewhere, though they are not racially different from the African-Liberians. Most authors have hesitated to define Americo-Liberians in ethnic terms, as a way of highlighting the qualitative differences between a civilised (Westernised) group and uncivilised (non-westernised) groups, a distinction which has its roots in the ethnocentricism of Western anthropology and modernisation theory. Instead, references to Americo-Liberians are in terms of class particularly because they exhibit the features of a distinct class — their efforts are geared towards perpetuating themselves as a dominant or privileged class. Yet, that class was one to which assimilated African-Liberians were admitted on terms set by the Americo-Liberians. Here then was a complex situation: a 'class' which contained ethnic elements, and which related with ethnic groups. The way we got around this problem was, following the analysis of similar situations in South Africa and United States of America, to regard the Americo-Liberians as constituting an ethnic category as well as a class and, again, following Gordon (1964) to formulate an ethclass framework for analysing the ethnic composition of Liberia.

There was an even more difficult aspect of the conceptualisation problem. Many authors analyse Americo-Liberian/African-Liberian distinctions only in historical terms, and the popular view is that by the 1970s, these categories were no longer relevant for analysing Liberian politics (Clapham 1989). For such authors, class categories became more relevant because strict Americo-Liberian/African-Liberian divisions no longer existed. The tenor of our formulations are clearly the opposite of this. We argued and demonstrated that the ruling class remained dominantly Americo-Liberian up until 1980 and, in Chapter 3, introduced the framework of hegemonic rule to ground this demonstration. The essence of hegemonic rule as it was presented is that, notwithstanding the assimilation and co-optation of African-Liberians into the ruling class, the ruling class remained Americo-Liberian as it was they who both controlled and determined the social order, the structure of the political process as articulated by the TWP, the allocative machinery, and the use of coercive forces. Largely for this reason, the African-Liberian section of the ruling class up until 1980 was dependent or comprador. It was not allowed to build independent power bases and could only continue to belong to the ruling class for as long as it accepted the suzerainty of the Americo-Liberians.

The coup of 1980 transformed the ethnic situation, necessitating, as Liebenow (1987) says, new frameworks of analysis. This transformation involved in the main, the turning of the focus on ethnic conflicts to the African-Liberian groups. This did not mean the end of Americo-Liberian ethclass as argued in Chapters 4 and 5. As a group, Americo-Liberians were only displaced from the governing elite position, not eliminated from the ruling class. Under Doe, they constituted the non-governing elite and continued their struggle for control of state power through collaboration with African-Liberian groups opposed to him. In this charged milieu, African-Liberians and Americo-Liberians became more or less equal competitors (meaning the days of hegemonic rule were gone), through given their numerical superiority (assuming they do not remain the factionalised elites that they are), the African-Liberians have numerical superiority on their side.[106] What the civil war showed, in part, was that the American-Liberian/African-Liberian cleavage has not melted. The next phase of the power struggle after the civil war would be devoted to how to work out power sharing formulas along the new lines, particularly because, as we argued in Chapter 5, the civil war provided the opportunity for some

---

106   The Americo-Liberians have, as we pointed out in the last chapter, the counterbalancing advantage of greater resources and international influence as well as intellectual and technocratic power.

cleavages which were previously latent to come to the fore. One of these was the Christian-Muslim cleavage.

The main conceptual challenge was to formulate a model which fitted in with the ethnic situation and was capable of accommodating its changing character. This was found in the internal colonialism model which, in its original formulation, is said to be most relevant in situations where internal colonialism is an on-going process, not one in which that process has been terminated, as was done in Liberian in 1980. The importance of the model and its relevance for our concern however lies in the fact that reactions to internal colonialism by the colonised, which may involve nationalist activity to the end of separation or succession (as Hechter and other classical internal colonialists argue) or overthrow of the coloniser (as in the Liberian case), as well as the aftermath of such nationalist activity (which, in Liberia, resulted in the civil war) are analysed as part of the internal colonialism process. In other words, like the effects of colonialism in Africa which far outlive the colonial situation (Ekeh 1983, 1986), the consequences of internal colonialism are not terminated when the internal colonialism situation is brought to an end. For a long period after then, it continues to dominate and determine political relationships and developments, and this much is demonstrated by the Liberian case. The internal colonialism model, with its epochal rather than episodic basis,[107] has enabled us to analyse the conflict situation in Liberia from 1820 to the civil war (1989-1992) as essentially aspects of the same process.

Although this study has been concerned with interethnic relations, the point that was made at the beginning and which featured prominently throughout the chapters is that ethnicity does not always exist in a pure form because ethnic cleavages are often intermeshed with other political cleavages like class, regionalism, religion and so on. The most important cross-cleavage in Liberia is class, and this study has shown, especially from the analysis of the civil war that ethnicity is, as Sklar (1967) described it long ago, 'a mask for class privilege'. Taylor's use of Gio/Mano ethnicity to pursue purely personal interest and Doe's mobilisation of the Krahn to sustain his personal rule are classical instances of elite-directed ethnicity. Regionalism, defined in terms of county identity and loyalty has also

---

107   Following Ekeh (1983), the epochal basis refers to the fact that the effects of an historical event far outlive the period during which it takes place, while an episodic basis means that the effects end with the termination of that event.

reinforced ethnicity because, for the most part, ethnic identities are coterminous with county identities. Nevertheless, there have been demands by minority ethnic groups for separate counties, and this informed Doe's creation of four new counties.[108] The wider implication of the fact that pure ethnicity is rare is that ethnicity is a situational phenomenon, which means that the analyst has to examine the actual conditions under which it is called into being. This is very important because conflicts which have the appearance of ethnic conflicts, like the civil war in Liberia may, on closer examination not be ethnic at all. Most conflicts in the country both before and after 1980 carried ethnic veils over purely personal interests.

Along the lines of these conceptual clarifications, this study proceeded to examine the rate of ethnic politics in Liberia in Chapters 2 to 5. The approach was basically historical, and the overall goal was to see the ways in which conflicts among the groups precipitated the civil war. In Chapter 2, we located the threshold of ethnicity within the foundation of the Liberian state as an exclusively Americo-Liberian state. In Chapter 3, we found that the Liberian state was forced by diverse circumstances — the claims of the French and British colonialists in neighbouring states to Liberian territory; the indictment by the League of Nations over the practice of internal slavery which nearly cost the country its independence; the increasing bankruptcy of the state which forced it to look towards the hinterland for exploitation of resources to back-up the open door policy; etc. — to incorporate hinterland Africans into the country, but that the leaders were not willing to let go Americo-Liberian oligarchy. This was why the unification initiatives of Tubman which were continued by Tolbert did not alter the political configuration, as was hoped. By refusing to expand the arena of political participation (by enfranchising all hinterlands adults, for example), which doubtlessly would have meant the end of hegemonic rule, the Americo-Liberians sowed the seeds of their own destruction.

In Chapter 4, we analysed the 1980 coup in terms of the overthrow of Americo-Liberian hegemonic rule, the ascendancy of African-Liberians to the position of governing elites, and the consequences of these events. The main consequence was the deterioration of relations amongst the previously united African-Liberians, especially, between the Krahn (and Mandingoes) and the Gio and Mano. These ethnic groups played the decisive roles in the

---

108   The demand of the Grebo of Grand Gedeh county for a separate county was not however responded to.

ethnic arena of Doe's military government up to 1985, and 'civilian' government from 1986 to 1989. Finally, in Chapter 5, we examined the civil war as a consequence of the historically located crisis of the Liberian state and, against the backdrop of the transformed ethnic terrain which led up to the war. Analysis revealed that although it had the trappings of an ethnic conflict, the civil war was the consequence of several contradictory forces in the Liberian society and the personal ambitions of Taylor, Doe, Johnson and other principal actors. The failure of the Liberian state to develop institutional checks to the emergence of personal rulership, which has been a regular feature of government since its inception (but more prominently since Tubman) in part explains the intransigence of Doe and the adventurism of Taylor.

The foregoing is a summary of the reaches and dimensions of our study. The major conclusions they permit are that:

1) control of state power will remain the major object of political competition in Liberia for a long time to come and, as long as this continues, the basic ethnic cleavages will remain;

2) any serious attempt at dealing with the problem of power sharing with a view to ameliorating ethnic politics has to address issues of economic weakness and foreign control as well as the issue of institution — building and observance;

3) in the immediate post-War period, a consociational type arrangement is necessary to stabilise the country and provide a basis for future discussions of power sharing; and

4) although alliance and compromise politics are most likely to dominate this period, the Americo-Liberians will continue to play deterministic roles when pitched against the factionalised African-Liberian elite.

The study has not sought to show that every conflict in Liberia, especially over control of state power, has an ethnic character or can only be explained in ethnic terms. Although, this may have appeared at some points to be the intention, because the approach was to decipher how much ethnic explanation could be proffered for conflict situations, the aim was really to discover those factors hidden by ethnic appearances. In this task, we dare say that the study has been successful because personal and class interests have emerged as the underlying basis of political conflicts. This was attributed to the decay of institutional checks to abuse and domination of political power which, in the first instance, gives ethnicity, clientelistic and prebendal politics full vent.

This study has not examined the forms of intra-Americo-Liberian and intra-group conflicts among African-Liberian groups largely because our concern was with macropolitics. We recognise the dangers in continuing to treat these entities as solidary or united groups, considering enormous sub-groups which made up the African-Liberian groups especially. In relation to the Americo-Liberians, it is important to see the internal divisions and conflicts that have emerged over the years and not continue to assume that they remain one entity. The civil war and the character of Taylor's ambitions clearly indicate the need for this kind of analysis. Hopefully, these would provide the basis for further research on the ethnic situation in Liberia. Part of what this study has achieved, we hope, is that it has hinted at the possible agenda for such research.

References

Adams, H, 1983, 'The Manipulation of Ethnicity: South Africa in Comparative Perspective', in *State Versus Ethnic Claims: African Policy Dilemma*, ed. by D, Rothchild and V, A, Olorunsola, Boulder, Westview Press.

Akpan, M, B, 1978, 'The Return to Africa — Sierra Leone and Liberia', *Tarikh*, Vol.5, No.4.

------------, 1981-82, 'Gola Resistance to Liberian Rule in the Nineteenth Century, 1835-1905', *Journal of the Historical Society of Nigeria*, Vol.11, Nos.1 & 2.

------------, 1982-83, 'Native Administration and Gola — Bandi Resistance in North-Western Liberia, 1905 — 1919', *Journal of Historical Society of Nigeria*, Vol. XI, Nos. 3 & 4.

------------, 1986, 'The Role of the Military in the History of Liberia, in *Liberia: Underdevelopment and Political Rule in a Peripheral Society*, ed. by R, Karpel *et. al.*, Hamburg, Institut for Afrika Kunde.

Anderson, R, E, 1952, *Liberia: America's African Friend*, Chapel Hill, University of North Carolina Press.

Anon, 1983, 'TWP Government, Stage Two', *West Africa*, 2 May.

Apthorpe, R, 1988, 'Does Tribalism Really Matter?', *Transition*, Vol. 7, No. 6.

Balandier, G, 1966, 'The Colonial Situation: A Theoretical Approach', in *Social Change: The Colonial Situation*, ed. by J, Wallerstein, New York, John Willey.

Beleky, L, P, 1973, 'The Development of Liberia', *Journal of Modern African Studies*, Vol. 2, No. 2.

Birch, A, H, 1978, 'Minority Nationalist Movement and Theories of Political Development', *World Politics*, Vol. XXX, No. 3.

Brass, P, 1965, *Factional Politics in an Indian State*, Berkeley, University of California Press.

Brooks, G, E, Jr., 1972, *The Kru Mariner in the Nineteenth Century: An Historical Compendium*, Newark, Liberian Studies Monograph Series, No. 1.

Brown, D, 1980, 'The Political Response to Immiseration: A Case Study of Rural Ghana', *Geneve-Afrique*, Vol. XVIII, No. 1.

Buell, R, L, 1965, *The Native Problem in Africa*, 2 Vols., London, Frank Cass.

Bullivant, B, M, 1984, *Pluralism: Cultural Maintenance and Evolution*, Clevedon, Multilingual Matters.

Cassell, C, A, 1970, *Liberia: History of the First African Republic*, New York, Fountainhead Publishers.

Chaudhuri, J, P, 1986, 'Liberia Under Military Rule (1980-1985), in *Liberia: Underdevelopment and Political Rule in a Peripheral Society*

Clapham, C, 1976, *Liberia and Sierra Leone: An Essay in Comparative Politics*, Cambridge, The University Press.

------------, 1978, 'Liberia', in *West African States: Failure and Promise*, ed. by J, Dunn, Cambridge, The University Press.

------------, 1988, 'The Politics of Failure: Clientelism, Political Instability and National Integration in Liberia and Sierra Leone', in *Private Patronage and Public Power: Political Clientelism in the Modern State*, ed. by C, Clapham, New York, St. Martins Press.

------------, 1989, 'Liberia', in *Contemporary West African States*, ed. by D, B, C, O'Brien, J, Dunn and R, Rathbone, Cambridge, The University Press.

Clifford, M, L, 1971, *The Land and People of Liberia*, Philadelphia and New York, J, B, Lippincott.

Clower, R, W, *et. al.*, 1966, *Growth Without Development: An Economic Survey of Liberia*, Evanston, North-Western University Press.

Cross, M, 1978, 'Colonialism and Ethnicity: A Theory and Comparative Case Study', *Ethnic and Racial Studies*, Vol. 1, No. 1.

D'Azevedo, W, L, 1962, 'Some Historical Problems in the Delineation of a Central West African Atlantic Region', *Annals of the New York Academy of Sciences*, Vol. XCVI.

------------, 1966, *The Artist Archetype in Gola Culture*, University of Nevada Desert Research Institute, Reprint No. 14.

------------, 1989, 'A Tribal Reaction to Nationalism', *Liberian Studies Journal*, Vol. 1, No. 2, Part 1.

------------, 1970, Part 3.

------------, 1970-71, Part 4.

Decalo, S, 1989, *Psychoses of Power: African Personal Dictatorships*, Boulder and London, Westview Press.

Dunn, D, E, and S, E, Holsoe, eds., 1985, *Historical Dictionary of Liberia*, London.

Ekeh, P, P, 1983, *Colonialism and Social Structure*, An Inaugural Lecture, Ibadan, The University Press.

------------, 1986, 'Development Theory and the African Predicament', *Africa Development*, Vol. II, No. 4.

------------, 1990, 'Social Anthropology and Two Contrasting Uses of Tribalism in Africa', *Comparative Studies in Society and History*, Vol. 32, No. 4.

Enloe, C, H, 1973, *Ethnic Conflict and Political Development*, Boston, Little Brown and Company.

Fraenkel, M, 1966, 'Social Change in the Kru Coast of Liberia', *Africa*, Vol. 36.

------------, 1964, *Tribe and Class in Monrovia*, London, Oxford University Press, for IAI.

Gay, J, and M, Cole, 1967, *The New Mathematics and an Old Culture: A Study of Learning Among the Kpelle of Liberia*, New York, Holt, Rhinehart and Winston.

Gray, J, H, *et. al.*, 1969, 'Language Map of Central Liberia', *Liberian Studies Journal*, Vol. 1, No. 2.

Gibbs, J, L, 1960, *Some Judicial Implications of Marital Instability Among the Kpelle* Unpublished, Ph.D. dissertation, Havard University.

------------, 1963, 'The Kpelle Moot: A Therapeutic Model for the Informal Settlement of Disputes', *Africa*, Vol. XXXIII, No. 1.

Givens, W, A, 1986, *Liberia: The Road to Democracy Under the Leadership of Samuel Kanyon Doe: The Policies and Public Statements of Dr. Samuel Kanyon Doe*, Bucks, Kensal Press.

Gonzates, P, 1965, 'Internal Colonialism and National Development', *Studies in Comparative International Development*, Vol. 1.

Gordon, M, 1964, *Assimilation in American Life*, New York, Oxford University Press.

Gramsci, A, 1971, *Selections from the Prison Notebooks of Antonio Gramsci* ed. by Q, Hoare and G, N, Smith, London, Lawrance and Wishart.

Greenberg, J, H, 1955, 'Studies in African Linguistic Classification', *Southwestern Journal of Anthropology*, Branford, Connecticut.

------------, 1963, 'The Language of Africa', *International Journal of American Linguistics* Vol. XXIX, No. 1.

Greenwall, H, J, and R, Wild, 1936, *Unknown Liberia*, London, Hutchinson.

Gurley, R, R, 1839, *Life of Jehudi Ashmun*, New York.

Hayman, A, I, and H, Preece, 1943, *Lighting Up Liberia*, New York, Creative   Press).

Hetcher, M, 1975, *Internal Colonialism: The Celtic Fringe in British National Development, 1536-1966*, London, Routledge and Kegan Paul.

Hetcher, M, 1978, 'Group Formation and the Cultural Division of Labour', *American Journal of Sociology*, Vol. 84, No. 2.

Henries, R, and O, Henries, 1966, *Liberia: The African Republic*, London, Macmillan.

Holsoe, S, E, and J, J, Lauer, 1976, 'Who are the Krahn/Guere and the Gio/Yacouba Ethnic Identifications Along the Liberia-Ivory Coast Border', *African Studies Review*, Vol. XXIX, No. 1.

------------ *et. al.*, 1969, 'Chiefdom and Clan Maps of Western Liberia', *Liberian Studies Journal*, Vol. 1, No. 2.

Huberich, C, H, 1947, *The Political and Legislative History of Liberia*, 2 Vols., New York, Central Book Company.

Hurstfield, J, 1978, 'Internal Colonialism: White, Black and Chicano Self-Conceptions', *Ethnic and Racial Studies*, Vol. 1, No. 1.

Ihonvbere, J, O, and T, Falola, 1984, 'Hegemony, Neo-colonialism and Political Instability in Contemporary Nigeria', *African Review*, Vol. II, No. 2.

Johnson, S, J, M, 1954, Tradition, History, Customary Laws, Moves, Folkways and Legends of the Vai Tribe, Monrovia, Bureau of Folkways.

------------, 1957, *Tradition, History and Folklore of the Grebo Tribe*, Monrovia, Bureau of Folkways.

------------, 1961, *Tradition, History and Folklore of the Gola Tribe in Liberia*, Monrovia, Bureau of Folkways.

------------, 1967, 'The Traditions, History and Folklore of the Pelle Tribe', *Liberian Studies Journal*, Vol. 1, No. 2.

Johnson, P, 1990, *Interview in West Africa*, 6-12 August.

Jones, H, B, 1962, *The Struggle for Political and Cultural Unification of Liberia*, Unpublished, Ph.D. dissertation, Northwestern University.

Jones, A, 1981, 'Who are the Vai?', *Journal of African History, Journal of Democracy*, Vol. 2, No. 4.

Kamara, S, 1986, 'The Role of the Putu Development Corporation (PUDECO) in Rural Conscientisation and Mobilisation in the 1970s', in *Liberia: Underdevelopment and Political Rule in a Peripheral Society*.

Kapper, *et. al.*, 1986, 'Foreward: Conditions in Liberia and their Reception', in *Liberia: Underdevelopment and Political Rule on a Peripheral Society*.

Karnga, A, 1926, *History of Liberia*, Liverpool.

Kup, A, P, 1960, 'An Account of the Tribal Distribution of Sierra Leone', London, Man.˙

Levine, V, T, 1976, 'Political Integration and the United Republic of Cameroon', in *The Search for National Integration in Africa*, ed. by D, R, Smock and K, Bentsi-Enchill, New York, The Free Press.

Liebenow, J, G, 1969, *Liberia: The Evolution of Privilege*, Ithaca and London, Cornell University Press.

----------, 1987, *Liberia: The Quest for Democracy*, Bloomington, University of Indiana Press.

Lowenkopf, M, 1976, *Politics in Liberia: The Conservative Road to Development*, Stanford, Hoover Institution Press.

Mafeje, A, 1971, 'The Ideology of Tribalism', *Journal of Modern African Studies*, Vol. 9, No. 2.

Mandaza, I, 1986, 'The State and Politics in the Post-White Settler Colonial Situation', in *Zimbabwe: The Political Economy of Transition, 1980-1986*, ed. by I, Mandaza, Dakar, CODESRIA.

Marinelli, L, A, 1964, *The Liberia: A Historical and Political Survey*, Pall Mall, for Africa Service Institute of New York.

McEvoy, F, D, 1977, 'Understanding Ethnic Realities Among the Grebo and Kru Peoples of West Africa', *Africa*, Vol. 47, No. 1.

Moniba, H, 1992, *Interview in West Africa*, 24 February-1 March.

Nicholson, N, K, 1972, 'The Factional Model and the Study of Politics', *Comparative Political Studies*, Vol. 1, No. 1.

Nnoli, O, 1978, *Ethnic Politics in Nigeria*. Enugu, Fourth Dimension).

----------, 1989. *Ethnic Politics in Africa*. Ibadan, Vintage Publishers, for AAPS.

Nyong'o, P, A, 1987, 'Popular Alliances and the State in Liberia, 1980-85', in *Popular Struggles for Democracy in Africa*, London, Zed and United Nations University.

Obatala, J, K, 1973, 'Liberia: The Meaning of Dual Citizenship', *Black Scholar*, July-August.

Osaghae, E, E. 1989, 'The Character of the State, Legitimacy Crisis and Social Mobilisation in Africa: An Explanation of Form and Character', *Africa Development*, Vol. XIV, No. 2.

----------, 1990, 'A Re-Examination of the Conception of Ethnicity in Africa as an Ideology of Inter-Elite Competition', *African Study Monograph*, Vol. 12, No. 1.

----------, 1992, 'Ethnicity in Africa or African Ethnicity: The Search for Contextual Understanding', in *Development Theories in an African Perspective*, ed. by U, Himmelstrand et. al., London, James Currey.

Otite, O, 1990. *Ethnic Pluralism and Ethnicity in Nigeria, With Comparative Notes*, Ibadan, Shaneson C.I.

Parkin, O, 1974, 'Congregational and Interpersonal Ideologies in Political Ethnicity', in *Urban Ethnicity*, ed. by A. Cohen, London, Tavistock.

Reece, J, E, 1979, 'Internal Colonialism: The Case of Brittany', *Ethnicity and Racial Studies*, Vol. 2, No. 3.

Roberts, T, D, et. al., 1972, *Area Handbook for Liberia*, Washington, The American University.

Sawyer, A, 1973, *Social Stratification and Orientations to National Development in Liberia*, Unpublished. Ph.D. Thesis, Northwestern University.

----------, 1990, 'Proprietary Authority and Local Administration', in *The Failure of the Centralised State: Institutions and Self-Governance in Africa*, ed. by J, S, Wunsch and D. Oluwu, Boulder, Westview.

----------, 1990, Interview in *African Concord*, 10 December.

Schmokel, W, W, 1969. 'Settler and Tribes: Origins of the Liberian Dilemma', in *West African History: Boston University Papers on Africa*, Vol. IV. ed. by D, F. McCalle et. al., New York, Friedrick, A, Praeger.

111

Schroder, G, and W, Korte, 1986, 'Samuel K, Doe, der People's Redemption Council und die Macht. Varlaufige Bernerkungen Zur Anatomie und Sozialpsychologie eines Putsches', in Liberia: Underdevelopment and Political Rule in a Peripheral Society.

Schroder, G, and D, Seibel, 1974, Ethnographic Survey of Southeastern Liberia: The Liberian Kran and the Sapo, Liberian Studies Monograph Series, No. 3.

Schulze, W, 1973, A New Geography of Liberia, London, Longman.

Schick, T, W, 1973, 'Liberia Reconsidered: A Reply to J, K, Obatala', Black Scholar, October.

Siegmann, W, 1969, Ethnographic Survey of Southeastern Liberia: Report on the Bassa, Robertsport, Tubman Centre of African Culture.

Simon, K, 1929, Slavery, London.

Simpson, C, L, 1961, The Memoirs of C, L, Simpson, London, Diplomatic Press.

Sklar, R, 1967, 'Ethnic Relations and Social Class'. Journal of Modern African Studies, Vol. 5, No. 1.

Slabbert, F, V, and D, Welsh, 1979, South Africa: Options: Strategies for Sharing Power, Cape Town and London, David Phillip and Rex Collings.

Smyke, R, J, 1983, 'Massaquoi of Liberia (1870-1938)', Geneve-Afrique, Vol. 21, No. 1.

Susukuu, 1978, Susukuu in Grand Gedeh County: A Response to Poverty, Monrovia.

Taryor, N, K, Snr., 1985, Justice: A Cry of My People, Chicago. Struggles Community Press.

Tipoteh, T, N, 1982, Democracy: The Cry of the Liberian People, Ostervala, O.J.

------------, 1985, 'Foreward', in Justice: A Cry of My People.

Townsend, E, R, 1959, President Tubman of Liberia Speaks, London, Consolidated Publications.

Tubman, W, B, 1986, 'Pluralism, Constitutionalism and Law in Africa: A Liberian View', in Democracy and Pluralism in Africa, ed. by D, Ronen, Boulder and London, Lynne Rienner and Hodder and Stoughton.

Van den Berghe, P, L, 1967, Race and Racism: A Comparative Perspective, New York, John Wiley.

Van der Kraaij, 1986, 'The Open Door Policy: Past, Present and Perspectives of the Liberian Concept of Foreign Investment'. in Liberia: Underdevelopment and Political Rule in a Peripheral Society.

Weinberg, L, 1964, 'Party Politics in West Africa', Geneve-Afrique, Vol. III, No. 2.

Williams, G, 1960, 'The Concept of 'Egemonia' in the thought of Antonio Gramsci', Journal of the History of Ideas, Vol. 21.

Wreh, T, 1976, The Love of Liberty: The Rule of President William, V.S. Tubman in Liberia 1944-1971, London, C, Hurst.

This monograph is an output of the Ethnic Conflicts in Africa Project, a CODESRIA MWG network.

www.ingramcontent.com/pod-product-compliance
Lightning Source LLC
Chambersburg PA
CBHW071136280326
41935CB00010B/1249